Devil's Advocates

DEVIL'S ADVOCATES is a series of books devoted to exploring the classics of horror cinema. Contributors to the series come from the fields of teaching, academia, journalism and fiction, but all have one thing in common: a passion for the horror film and a desire to share it with the widest possible audience.

'The admirable Devil's Advocates series is not only essential – and fun – reading for the serious horror fan but should be set texts on any genre course.'
Dr Ian Hunter, Reader in Film Studies, De Montfort University, Leicester

'Devil's Advocates critiques on individual titles... offer bracingly fresh perspectives from passionate writers. The series will perfectly complement the BFI archive volumes.' **Christopher Fowler,** *Independent on Sunday*

'Devil's Advocates has proven itself more than capable of producing impassioned, intelligent analyses of genre cinema... quickly becoming the go-to guys for intelligent, easily digestible film criticism.' ***Horror Talk.com***

Also available in this series

A Girl Walks Home Alone at Night Farshid Kazemi
Black Sunday Martyn Conterio
The Blair Witch Project Peter Turner
Blood and Black Lace Roberto Curti
The Blood on Satan's Claw David Evans-Powell
The Cabin in the Woods Susanne Kord
Candyman Jon Towlson
Cannibal Holocaust Calum Waddell
Cape Fear Rob Daniel
Carrie Neil Mitchell
The Company of Wolves James Gracey
The Conjuring Kevin J. Wetmore Jr.
The Craft Miranda Corcoran
Creepshow Simon Brown
Cruising Eugenio Ercolani & Marcus Stiglegger
The Curse of Frankenstein Marcus K. Harmes
Daughters of Darkness Kat Ellinger
Dawn of the Dead Jon Towlson
Dead of Night Jez Conolly & David Bates
The Descent James Marriot
The Devils Darren Arnold
Don't Look Now Jessica Gildersleeve
The Evil Dead Lloyd Haynes
The Fly Emma Westwood
Frenzy Ian Cooper
Halloween Murray Leeder
House of Usher Evert Jan van Leeuwen
I Walked With a Zombie Clive Dawson
In the Mouth of Madness Michael Blyth
IT Chapters One and Two Alissa Burger
It Follows Joshua Grimm
Ju-on The Grudge Marisa Hayes
Let the Right One In Anne Billson
M Samm Deighan
Macbeth Rebekah Owens
The Mummy Doris V. Sutherland
Nosferatu Cristina Massaccesi
The Omen Adrian Schober
Peeping Tom Kiri Bloom Walden
Poltergeist Rob McLaughlin
Possession Alison Taylor
Re-Animator Eddie Falvey
Repulsion Jeremy Carr
Saw Benjamin Poole
Scream Steven West
The Shining Laura Mee
Shivers Luke Aspell
The Silence of the Lambs Barry Forshaw
Suspiria Alexandra Heller-Nicholas
The Texas Chain Saw Massacre James Rose
The Thing Jez Conolly
Trouble Every Day Kate Robertson
Twin Peaks: Fire Walk With Me Lindsay Hallam
The Wicker Man Steve A. Wiggins
Witchfinder General Ian Cooper

Devil's Advocates

The Woman in Black

Mark Fryers
and
Marcus K. Harmes

Acknowledgements

The writers would like to thank the editors Christabel Scaife and Ally Lee and the editorial board at LUP for all their help and support on the project, as well as Kate Egan for championing the proposal. Thanks especially to John Atkinson for steering and nurturing the project in the early stages: we hope it's a worthy testimony as your final project for Auteur/LUP. We also thank the peer reviewers of the proposal and the completed manuscript for their useful suggestions.

Thanks also to Wendy Thirkettle and the team at the Isle of Man Archives for their invaluable assistance. Special thanks to birdwatcher Jim Jewson for identifying all the bird sounds heard in the production!

A big thanks also to Assistant Director Bill Kirk for his fascinating and invaluable insights into the making of the film, and to former BBC cameraman Martin Kempton who similarly offered illuminating insights into the technical and aesthetic aspects of broadcast studio recording.

First published in 2025 by
Liverpool University Press
4 Cambridge Street
Liverpool
L69 7ZU

Series design: Nikki Hamlett at Cassels Design
Set by Carnegie Book Production, Lancaster

All rights reserved. No part of this publication may be reproduced in any material form (including photocopying or storing in any medium by electronic means and whether or not transiently or incidentally to some other use of this publication) without the permission of the copyright owner.

British Library Cataloguing-in-Publication Data
A catalogue record for this book is available from the British Library
ISBN hardback: 9781836243472
ISBN paperback: 9781836243489
eISBN PDF: 9781836243625

Contents

Figures vii

Introduction 1

Interlude: The Story 7

Chapter 1: 'I felt a strange sensation, excitement mingled with alarm':
    Production, Reception, and TV Horror 9

Chapter 2: 'Vying with one another to tell the horridist, most spine-chilling tale':
    Authorship and Adaptation 21

Chapter 3: 'She has found a way to make me hear their calamity in the marshes':
    Aurality, Time, and Technology 49

Chapter 4: 'Just a house, on the marshes': Landscapes, Seascapes, and Horror 63

Chapter 5: 'Mr Drablow was a China trader, he died out East':
    Colonialism and National Identity 83

Chapter 6: 'I won't be feared of my own Kin': Ghostly Children and
    Maternal Hatred 95

Conclusion 105

Bibliography 107

Figures

Figure 1. A moment of pure terror, shot 'in camera' 17

Figure 2. Nine Lives Causeway with its serpentine qualities 47

Figure 3. The wax disc recorder is an integral part of Kneale's narrative 56

Figures 4 and 5. Framing in 4:3 (Figure 4) and 16:9 (Figure 5) – both indicate
    verticality in the composition. In both, the landscape is
    equally significant 72

Figure 6. Colonial objects in Eel Marsh nursery 93

Figure 7. Janet poised to break through into the domestic realm 99

Figure 8. Conclusive finale as Arthur and family are fatally drawn into the
    woman's web 105

Introduction

On the evening of Christmas Eve 1989, viewers in Britain sat down to watch a film with a title that sounded innocuous enough. *The Woman in Black* could well have been a romantic costume drama. It was a costume drama certainly and a beautifully detailed period piece. However, the woman herself was a shocking aural and visual creation with terrifying impact. *The Woman in Black* (hereafter *TWIB*), both the television film and the titular character, live on in popular memory as a notably frightening story in the tradition of spine-chilling Christmas ghost stories on British television.

The woman herself has only a few minutes of screen time and has no dialogue, but she lingers as a ghastly memory for one particular scene towards the end of the story. A young man is sleeping restlessly and awakes, but awakes into a nightmare. Above him, bearing down on him, is a revoltingly perfect synthesis of makeup, acting, editing, music, and timing as a black spectre appears, leering and screeching. The scene must rank as one of the most memorable cuts to an advertisement break in British television history – indeed, as devotee Mark Gatiss suggests, 'the most necessary ad break in the history of television' (DVD commentary, 2020). This moment comes towards the end of the one-hour-and-42-minute television movie and the apparition is the most forcefully terrifying as well as the most audible and physical of the appearances the woman makes throughout the story.

TWIB was Nigel Kneale's adaptation of Susan Hill's 1983 novella. The novella had already (in 1987) been adapted imaginatively for the stage to great acclaim and would again in 2012 receive adaptation as a successful horror movie by the revived Hammer Productions. It was also adapted as a BBC Radio serial in 1993 and again in 2004. But the 1989 television movie perhaps eclipses all these not only in how frightening it is but how well remembered it remains.

On Christmas Eve, viewers tuned to the ITV network started watching *TWIB* at 9:30pm. It was part of an eclectic line-up on ITV that evening including Harry Secombe presenting *Highway* from Durham Cathedral, and *TWIB* was immediately preceded by a showing of the 1989 film *Pied Piper* with Peter O'Toole. The broadcast was followed by a church service from the parish church in Lockerbie, perhaps to provide spiritual comfort for terrified viewers.

The audience will also have seen many familiar faces from television in the cast for *TWIB* including Bernard Hepton, known by then for *Colditz* (and the 1970 pagan horror *Robin Redbreast*, from the *Play for Today* series), David Ryall from *Bless Me, Father*, and David Daker from *Boon*. Other familiar faces rounded out the cast including John Cater, William Simons, John Franklyn Robbins, and Fiona Walker, actors with many decades of experience and multiple television credits. As Arthur Kidd, Wise cast Adrian Rawlins in an early and rare leading role as the naive solicitor and family man whose life is destroyed by his visit to Eel Marsh House. Direction was by the experienced and award-winning Herbert Wise, who in turn recruited some up-and-coming talent including the composer Rachel Portman. In the awards season for 1990 *TWIB* did especially well in terms of its production and technical aspects, scoring BAFTA nominations for design, makeup, film sound, and Portman's score.

Although produced for television, *TWIB* demands that the similarities and differences between horror films produced for cinema and television be examined. (Its cinematic nature will further be contextualised by insights from the Kneale Archive on the Isle of Man and from the memories of its first assistant director.) Produced on 16mm film and with extensive location shooting and sophisticated sound design, and adapted for the screen by noted screenwriter (especially of horror and fantasy) Nigel Kneale, *TWIB* is an important cultural landmark in televisual horror film production.

Both at the time and since, it is clear that *TWIB* is something special. Some of that sense of exceptionality comes from long inaccessibility. There was a repeat in 1994 (on Christmas Day, in keeping with its original broadcast as a seasonal horror) but never again. As Andrew Male noted in the *Guardian* in 2020, this cult favourite simply disappeared. There was a limited VHS release (exclusively through the retailer WH Smith) and the DVD release is only recent. Indeed, the truth behind this disappearance is prosaic, as the yielding of film/televisual rights in 1988 was contingent on not distracting away from the West End play, which was beginning to garner its own momentum as the film went into production (i.e., they should be able to coexist – Murray, 2017: 268).

The film also became subject of 'fearful nostalgia' – that is, a nostalgia either for texts which scared us during childhood (we are both compelled towards their giddy thrills and equally repelled by the memories of being scared as a child) or those that continue to haunt us. Mark Gatiss fondly recalls the film (and contributes to the DVD commentary). In his documentary *A History of Horror with Mark Gatiss* (2010), he shared memories of staying up late to watch double bills of horror films and that Alan G. Frank's book *The Movie Treasury: Horror Movies* was a treasured text for him. Such was the popularity of another book, Usborne's *The World the Unknown: All About Ghosts*, that it has recently been reissued with a foreword by Gatiss's *The League of Gentleman* co-creator Reece Shearsmith. Gatiss's fondness for all things horror have informed his work and in particular, he has carried the torch for *A Ghost Story for Christmas* by renewing the annual Christmas adaptation of M. R. James (as well as his own, original creations) since *Crooked House* in 2008. *TWIB* is one of the original inspirations for these and part of a lineage of providing seasonal chills.

Absence enables legends to grow and accessibility can dampen reputations. But *TWIB* does not disappoint and lives up to the legend that accumulated in the years it was locked away in the archives. Scholars, critics, fans, and practitioners all agree that it is up there with Kneale's best work. Even Kneale himself was happy with the result: 'It's pretty good, actually, it was perfectly well done – good acting and direction' (in Murray, 2017: 266) – although tellingly, in a letter looking back on his career, he omits it entirely from his biography (Letter, 31 March 1999). Kneale biographer Andy Murray describes it as 'something of a masterpiece, one of Kneale's best-realised adaptations' (2017: 265). Author Stephen Gallagher suggests it is a 'solid and cinematic piece of drama' (in Murray, 2017: 266–7) – the use of 'cinematic' will form a central interrogation of this book. *Ghost Stories* (2017) writer Jeremy Dyson praises Kneale's 'brilliant touches' (in Murray, 2017: 267). Andy Nyman, who debuted as an actor in the film (as office clerk, Jackie) praised the 'brilliance' of director Herbert Wise (DVD commentary, 2020). For commentator Kim Newman, it is 'an impressive piece of work' (in Murray, 2017: 268) while for Mark Gatiss, it is 'marvellous… immaculate' (in Murray, 2017: 267).

In a larger sense, it is part of a broadcasting history of 'event television' that began to dissipate in the multi-channel and streaming era ('a sense of occasion' as Andy Nyman describes – DVD commentary, 2020). In commentary, Mark Gatiss, Andy Nyman, and Kim Newman all recall watching the original with their families, with abiding memories of their own and their parents' stunned reactions to the film: a testimony to the ability of the broadcast era to forge intimate, domestic, and familial viewing contexts that produce similar personal memories.

The film is part of the customs and boundary rituals of the broadcast era – watching with family, but also to a longer cultural tradition of festive ghost stories, which has its roots in the oral tradition (see Johnston, 2015a on this) of presenting a 'ghost story for Christmas'. As such, and for many more reasons explored, *TWIB* is a text that is an important part of cultural history, especially within its British context of production and reception.

This book

This book, the first from the Devil's Advocates series to appreciate a made-for-TV movie in detail, aims to make the case for the artistic and cultural merit of texts like *TWIB* which have been overlooked, in part due to their status as a text in-between cinematic and televisual appreciation. Using a combination of close textual reading, archival research, critical reception material, analysis of the film's production process, and interviews with its personnel, the book will build a case for the artistic and cultural relevance of *TWIB* as distinct from its literary and theatrical antecedents. Each chapter will consider ways the cinematic and the televisual exist within *TWIB*.

Chapter One examines the film's reception and the aesthetics and impact of its production design. The second chapter then looks at the creative adaptive process of turning a pseudo-period novella into a film, examining the key creative players, the writer of the novel, its adaptor, and the director. The previously underappreciated skill of televisual sound design, both in its technical and aesthetic rendering, will lead the analysis of the third chapter. The impact of landscape and setting in the fourth chapter then leads to the consideration of the adaptation's engagement with colonialism in the fifth chapter, which itself will lead to a sustained analysis of the role of women and children in the final chapter.

These chapters therefore consider *TWIB* from multiple angles from its themes to its production and as a film with the expansive aesthetic qualities and thematic and cultural complexities of cinematic horror. Furthermore, we examine the film in relation to multiple horror contexts – of the gothic, landscape, gender, imperialism, and global horror contexts within wider historical, cultural, social, and political discourses. We begin and continue by considering this work as presenting its own version of this story, in particular in how Kneale created a heightened catastrophe on a cinematic scale. Kneale also contributed the horrific resonances of sound, enabling a notably cinematic aspect of this film. In the same way, Kneale's link to sonic aesthetics in his earlier work provides further contextual consideration as cinematic film modulates to television, especially his use of and emphasis on technology as a conduit for terror. The use of haunted/doomed landscapes also sits within several traditions of horror film and literature.

By the end of our study, we intend to have categorised the text as part of a broader conception of both horror and history, with consideration of the colonialist themes as pointing to the dialectic that horror is history, and history is horror in the manner in which, within specific readings, they can be read as one and the same. As such, the book shows this work breaking its bounds as purely 'television horror' and that these boundaries are not discrete. First, a brief interlude sets the scene with the ghostly events taking place in Crythin Gifford.

Interlude: The Story

TWIB is the creative achievement of three major figures in British writing and television, being written by Susan Hill, adapted by Nigel Kneale, and directed by Herbert Wise. Adapting Hill's work, Kneale scripted a story of a young solicitor called Kidd (renamed from Kipps in the novella) sent to the remote Eel Marsh House, reached by a causeway, to finalise the probate on the estate of the late Alice Drablow. He attends her funeral with Mr Pepperell, a lawyer. Local landowner Sam Toovey, whom he meets on the train on the way down, cautions Kidd against staying in the house. The house is intimidatingly sinister and Kidd is increasingly unnerved by his environment, including the strangely lifeless and joyless outlook of the local people in Crythin Gifford and the suspiciously large number of children's graves in the churchyard.

What he sees and hears around him further unnerves him. He has a spectral vision of a woman in black who looks seriously ill and dresses in old-fashioned mourning dress, and encounters doors that open and objects that move by themselves. He hears ghostly sounds on the causeway and, from playing wax cylinders, he hears the voice of Alice Drablow recounting her own eerie experiences as a ghost terrorised her at night. Using the same wax cylinder, Kidd adds his own voice to this aural nightmare. Kidd learns that Mrs Drablow's late sister Janet (renamed from Jennet in the novella) is the malevolent woman in black. Janet had a child out of wedlock who died on the causeway. Janet now haunts the house and the area. Frightened beyond endurance, first by the ghostly destruction of a child's nursery and then by the screaming apparition of the titular woman, Kidd begins to lose his sanity, loses his job, and ultimately loses his life to the malevolence of the woman in black when he, his wife, and their child are crushed by a tree and drown.

Chapter One: 'I felt a strange sensation, excitement mingled with alarm': Production, Reception, and TV Horror

Prior to its broadcast, notices and stories in the press primed audiences to expect a scary viewing experience in the Christmas Eve tradition. Primarily, that expectation was because of the involvement of Nigel Kneale, less so because of Susan Hill's source text. Kneale remained active in the 1980s writing original works for television and adaptations of other people's works. Repeats of his older works kept his most famous creations in the public eye, including 1988 and 1989 repeats of the Hammer film adaptations *The Quatermass Xperiment* and *Quatermass and the Pit*.

The *Nottingham Evening Post* connected the impending broadcast of *TWIB* to two major televisual reputations, the BBC's ghost stories for Christmas and Kneale's *Quatermass* serials. First noting that 'no Christmas would be complete without a ghost story', the notice continued the television film was by the man who 'wrote *Hallowe'en III* and the original *Quatermass* serials, so should know what he's doing in the hackle-raising department' (23 December 1989: 56). The *Visitor* likewise noted 'Nigel Kneale, who wrote the original *Quatermass* serials for television, returns to the field of the chiller in this ghost story for Christmas' (21 December 1989: 29). Local connections including star Adrian Rawlin's midlands upbringing prompted the *Birmingham Mail* to cover the production in detail. Among other details such as Rawlin's reported encounter with ghosts and the interest of guest star Pauline Moran in astrology, the report again reinforced the significance of Kneale, the writer who 'was the originator of the *Quatermass Experiment* which so startled 1950s' audiences' (14 December 1989: 28). Similarly, *The Times* selected it for their recommended viewing: 'a handsomely mounted ghost story for Christmas from television veteran Nigel (Quatermass) Kneale by way of Susan Hill's book' (23 December 1989: 36).

Reviews from the time suggest that the film served its purpose in eliciting chills, as well as being welcomed for keeping up the tradition of providing a televisual 'ghost story for Christmas'. Richard Last in the *Daily Telegraph*, stated:

What we do have – rarest of treats – was a genuine Christmas Eve ghost story. Susan Hill, who wrote the book on which Central based The Woman in Black (ITV) is not M. R. James, and even Herbert Wise, who directed, does not command the slow, uncoiling terror of Leslie Megahey's classic horror productions… As we approached the climatic moments of Miss Hill's tale in the eerie house on the marshes, my scalp hair prickled in the approved manner and I was extremely glad that the dog had not gone to church with the rest of the family. (27 December 1989: 14)

Meanwhile, Patrick Stoddart in the *Sunday Times* suggested that it was a standout broadcast in a Christmas period cursed with a dearth of original programming with a seasonal flavour: 'ITV does at least provide us with a good ghost story tonight – a Nigel Kneale adaptation of Susan Hill's The Woman in Black' (24 December 1989: 23). This was echoed by Philip Purser in the *Daily Telegraph*: 'The best chance of something out of the ordinary on the main channels comes from new drama – The Woman in Black, a ghostly story from Susan Hill with screenplay by Nigel Kneale' (22 December 1989: 19), while John Dugdale in the *Listener* suggested that opting for the 'veteran' team of Kneale and Wise produced a result that was 'handsome, unflashy and highly effective' (21 December 1989: 48). One dissenting voice was James Saynor, also writing in the *Listener* (4 January 1990: 38), who wrote that it was 'not particularly unexpected' and helmed in 'relentlessly half-timbered fashion'. Perhaps reflecting the propensity for larger budgeted, gore-filled Hollywood (and other) horror movies in the 1980s, Saynor remarked, 'someone who's spent any time at the cinema over the past 15 years would have been hard-pushed to suffer serious discombobulation' (1990: 38). It would seem that the audience felt very differently, however.

Horror on television

Reviewers therefore expected and got a horror film. For numerous reasons, horror on television has presented a problematic paradigm. For Abbott and Jowett, 'TV horror exists as a nexus of often conflicting influences and factors that have shaped the genre' (2013: xiii), while Matt Hills suggests that censorship and other factors have dissuaded producers from identifying programming as horror, thus making it somewhat 'invisible' (2005, in Abbott and Jowett, 2013: 17).

Yet, psychological, literary, and gothic horror (by the latter two of which terms *TWIB* may accurately be described), if not graphic horror, have traditionally found a natural and thriving home on the small screen. Helen Wheatley, in her study of gothic television, distinguishes between terror and horror on television and concludes that 'These programmes demonstrated a clear consciousness of their domestic reception context, not merely in their repeated return to the home as dramatic location' (2006: 28). Horace Newcomb conceived the notion of televisual 'intimacy' as a defining feature of televisual address (1974). Laurie Schulze extended this point, suggesting that 'the TV movie has fashioned an aesthetic from its limitations… TV movies extend the principle of intimacy into their narrative material as well' (Schulze, 1990: 360 in Stone, 2017: 615–16). Catherine Johnson (2005) applies this concept to consider the mixture of 'intimacy and spectacle' seen in pioneering works of 'telefantasy', primarily Nigel Kneale's serial *The Quatermass Experiment* (1953).

The intimacy of television and its domestic context can heighten the dramatic effects for horrific content that similarly haunts the spaces of its reception environment. Horror perhaps offers both an intensified and horrific intimacy on the small screen. It is also the medium through which most horror films were seen, especially by audiences too young to view them at the cinema. As will be explored, it is an aesthetic of intimacy that helps illuminate the horrific potential of *TWIB*.

Likewise, the made-for-TV movie has also been traditionally viewed as inferior to its cinematic counterpart. As Nora Stone points out, 'The made-for-TV movie has often been represented one-dimensionally, a bad object to be judged against "real" films that play in theaters' (2017: 615), and 'defining a media form by its exhibition site and assumed audience ignores the dynamic shape of the media industry' (2017: 616). Thus, the made-for-TV horror film may be said to suffer from a doubly degraded reputation.

Nevertheless, those made-for-TV films that progressed beyond their boundaries on the small screen were predominantly horror films, with Steven Spielberg's *Duel* (1971) being the most successful when released theatrically (with extra content produced for European theatrical release). The vampire-detective film *The Night Stalker* (1972) and the horrific apocalyptic drama *The Day After* (1983) were also among the most successful (Stone, 2017). This book, therefore, makes a case for the defence of made-for-TV horror films, and seeks to suggest that they merit the type of artistic and cultural appreciation made throughout this volume and previously across the Devil's Advocates series on cinematic horror.

The made-for-television horror movie as a genre has a longer series of American antecedents. Throughout the 1970s, American network television produced horrors made especially for television. Many featured major stars, including Olivia de Havilland (*The Screaming Woman*, 1972) and Kim Novak (*Satan's Triangle*, 1975). Others remain well remembered as notable productions in their own right, including *Gargoyles* (1972) and *Satan's School for Girls* (1973), while Guillermo del Toro co-wrote and produced the 2010 cinematic remake of *Don't Be Afraid of the Dark* (1973).

Being made for network television necessarily limited what program makers could show in terms of gore and violence, and the films tend to be suggestive and allusive rather than direct. Matt Hills suggests that networks often disguised horror as something else (in Abbott and Jowett, 2013: 17). In the UK, the ghost story was allowed to thrive, but these were more often conflated with the respectable, historical, literary, and costume drama – all categories that could describe *TWIB*.

Their budgets were constraints, but network horror films could use ingenious makeup and special effects (*Gargoyles* won a Primetime Emmy for makeup effects) and be major broadcasting events timed to appropriate moments in the calendar such as Halloween. Over a hundred made-for-television horror films make the 1970s a 'golden age' for horror on the American small screen, with works that traversed style and genre from adaptations of literary classics to works set in the present day. John Kenneth Muir notes a very American cultural inflection as influencing their production and popularity, with the routine broadcasting of violent Vietnam War footage causing a 'turn toward darkness' which fuelled this cavalcade of horror on television (2012: 27).

British horror also existed on the small screen as well as the big. Television in the 1970s proliferated with horror and supernatural themes, including *Dead of Night* (1972), *Beasts* (1976), and *Supernatural* (1977), which were shows preceded by others including *Tales of Mystery and Imagination* (1966) and succeeded by more including *Hammer House of Horror* (1980). Most were anthologies and not television movies, most episodes being between 50 minutes and an hour in length. Settings could range from historical periods to the present day, and scripts could be original works or adaptations of venerable ghost-story writers such as J. Sheridan le Fanu and M. R. James.

The production team commissioned Nigel Kneale to adapt the novella of *TWIB* into a script. Kneale had been writing professionally for television since 1951, when he produced a script for the crime series *Web*. Adapting the works of both living and dead writers is a major element of Kneale's writing career. While best remembered and lauded for the startling originality of the *Quatermass* serials and other original works such as *The Stone Tape* and *Beasts*, some of Kneale's most acclaimed writing is as the adaptor of other people's work. Complicating the common perception of Kneale as a science fiction writer, his adaptations for *Look Back in Anger* (1959) and *The Entertainer* (1960) are by any measure some of Kneale's most acclaimed works. For both he received a BAFTA nomination for his screenplay and both situated him in the domain of kitchen sink drama then prevalent in British film and theatre, far removed from spaceships and monsters.

He adapted a well-received version of *Wuthering Heights* for the BBC's *Sunday-Night Theatre* in 1953 and most contentious but equally celebrated was his script for the BBC's *Nineteen Eighty-Four* in 1954, which caused a much discussed and analysed controversy. Adapting other people's works remained a mainstay of his writing career, taking him across an astonishing diversity of genres, including his script for the naval adventure *HMS Defiant* (1962, from Frank Tilsley's novel) and historical drama such as *The Cathedral* (1952 teleplay based on a story by Hugh Walpole).

His next work after *TWIB* was to adapt Kingsley Amis's *Stanley and the Women* into a miniseries. Far removed from chilling ghost stories, he adroitly turned Amis's novel about the domestic and mental-health issues of an advertising executive into a four-part miniseries set in present-day London. As an adaptor, Kneale was both highly effective and high handed. He acknowledged how far he deviated from the source text when adapting Bernard Cornwell's *Sharpe's Gold* and stated he diverged from the story after the first ten pages as he found his own ideas were far more interesting (Murray, 2017: 276).

His writing career has seen him lauded as among the most significant writers in British television history, whose creation of *Quatermass* came at a critical moment in the development of television as a new medium, and where his understanding of the dramatic structures and storytelling modes appropriate for television were central to its creative development. One strain of significance is the televisuality inherent to Kneale's work. Kneale traverses television and film. Kneale outlined this process himself, moving from a writer of short stories and radio scripts to television: 'I wanted to make my work more visual' (Murray, 2017: 35). The *Quatermass* serials became financially successful movies, in some instances with Kneale as adaptor of his own work, the first major TV production to be adapted for film and, according to Veronica Taylor, Kneale was 'the first TV writer to become a household name' (BFI Programme notes, March 2000: 40). The way that not only his writing in general but even the same stories and characters modulated from television to cinema caution us against seeing any binary distinction between the big screen and the small. It is here we find *TWIB*.

Making *The Woman in Black*: an insider remembers

Before moving to the studies offered in the following chapters, the production history of *TWIB* provides valuable context for studying the work as both a film and a television experience. The themes within *TWIB* are myriad but just as fascinating is the work of a time-poor but experienced team working against the odds and against the clock to produce high-quality work with limited resources. Making *TWIB* was a labour of love. Director Herbert Wise and his cast and crew worked over winter at bleak Essex locations, starting early, working in darkness, and as we shall see, in some instances paying from their own pocket to make the film as good as possible.

The production company shortened an eight-week production period to six weeks. There was never quite enough money. The conditions were ghastly and the cast and crew froze in inhospitable weather during winter. While she looks terrifying on screen as the titular woman, in reality Pauline Moran was shivering with cold when filming her scenes. Other members of the cast suffered odd privations in the pursuit of excellence, among the oddest being the quantity of sausage meat routinely smeared on Adrian Rawlins to encourage the dog to interact with him. The locations placed strain on cast and crew. In the drama the fact people must reach the house by and can be cut off from a causeway is central to the plot. In reality, the same thing happened to the production team: as first assistant director Bill Kirk recalls, 'the island was reached by a tidal causeway, so the schedule had to allow for varying tide times, often resulting in early Unit calls and critical wrap times to get off the island before the tide cut us off'.

The director Herbert Wise, though, assembled and inspired a tight-knit cast and crew, one Bill Kirk praises as a 'formidable crew', 'unfazed and committed despite several unforeseen setbacks we were hit with'. With clear leadership, Wise set the style and tone of all aspects of the production from design to performances and everything else in between. As is typical, Wise received support and collaborated with a first assistant director, in this instance Bill Kirk. Now retired, Kirk's lengthy career in television has included further work on period drama including *Poirot* and *Monsieur Reynard*, as well as further work with Wise on *Class Act* in 1994 and 1995. He was also a fan of Kneale's work, including *The Stone Tape*. *TWIB* was relatively early in his career and may have been something of a baptism of fire, with Kirk as first assistant given responsibilities for planning and coordination of 'what, at the time, appeared to be an almost impossible schedule'. In retrospect, Kirk remembers the amazement of the third assistant director, Cliff Lanning, one shared by other members of the crew: '"How did we pull that off?" We started with a preliminary schedule of eight five-day weeks, which due to pressures from the production company and the financiers, was reduced to six six-day weeks with little or no respite for Company/Unit moves or, indeed, any latitude for errors or omissions'.

In part, they pulled it off because Wise ran a tight ship, and by the time cameras rolled he had made explicit his vision and requirements to all the different production departments. 'In pre-production, all departments had an allotted day with him alone, where he would go through the script in fine detail, outlining exactly what he wanted to see and expect from their expertise'.

If nothing else, this information provides a corrective to a commonly held assumption (at least, historically) that broadcast television was less of a medium populated by creative 'auteurs' with a distinct 'vision' than its cinematic counterpart. *TWIB* is a notably visually authoritative and authentic-looking production. The carefully chosen locations ground it in a plausible physical reality, and the historic village and church used meant the design department needed only minor production design changes to turn the streetscapes of the 1980s into those of the early twentieth century. Further visual authority and authenticity come from the physical directness of the filming. There is only one special effect in the film, which is the superimposing of a glass plate of the house in Twyford to make it appear as though Arthur is travelling towards it on the causeway.

There was also only one set built, the solicitor's office (at the Lee International Studios in Wembley) which had to be set on fire and nearly destroyed at the conclusion of the film. Other than that, Wise's cameras capture real things, people, and scenes. That most memorable of scenes, the woman bearing down on Kidd as he awakes, was meticulously planned. The team achieved it all 'in camera' through the most physical of means and not with special effects. 'The apparition of the Woman was filmed on location. It is not a "special effect" but rather the intelligent use of the dolly, camera, makeup, costume, and a small wind machine. And I do not forget Pauline's terrifying character performance,' says Kirk. Its potency makes it so well remembered, and the coordinated combination of all these resources, technical and actorly, left its mark on the crew filming it. Kirk still remembers the impact it had on everyone there: 'I remember when Mr Wise said "Cut" after the take, which I believe was the only one, we were all silent for some time. I often wonder if it was more terrifying on set than in the film'. Intriguingly, the drama critic Kim Newman remembers the impact of the woman in terms of 'after-effects, a mood that continued after the film ended. You wake up next morning, Christmas Day, you're still scared' (Male, 2020). Small wonder, given their own work unsettled the crew.

Another factor working to the advantage of a time-poor crew was the completeness and professionalism of Kneale's script. Barring 'an occasional grammatical correction or a re-emphasis of a character trait, the script remained the same document I had analysed and scheduled, making it easier to plan and think ahead for all concerned', a memory confirmed as we shall soon see by the drafts in the Isle of Man Archives. Kneale was only an occasional visitor to the production but Kirk recollects a productive professional relationship between writer and director.

As would be typical, from time to time setbacks occurred, as will plague any production. The first rushes were scratched in the laboratory, necessitating re-shoots that put pressure on an already shortened shooting schedule. Underpinning the production was skill in brilliant improvisation to make up for lost time. As first assistant, Kirk needed and possessed the ability to re-do schedules on the spot, to accommodate disasters such as scratched negatives.

Figure 1. A moment of pure terror, shot 'in camera'.

But less typical are challenges that came about because, behind the scenes, company executives were struggling and failing to make up their mind on one critical question: were they making a feature film, on a feature-film budget and schedule, or not? This dithering had technical and ultimately creative implications. In technical terms, it meant that Wise's eight weeks of production lost a fortnight, the company scaling it back to a more modest six weeks. It also had technical implications for the technology used. As Kirk remembers, 'After the first week of rushes, we were asked what the possibilities of reverting to 35mm would be and retaking the previous footage. However, the executives baulked at the idea of any additional expenditure'. Their lack of faith is curious, as not only had the novella been a creative and commercial success, but there was also a current acclaimed theatre adaptation, and the production team was experienced and mature. In fact, the technology was a slight mishmash, with most of the work made with 35mm film, but the plate of the house made on a 35S Mitchell camera.

There were also creative implications, ones at the core of this volume's study of *TWIB* as a television work with the feel and scope of a feature film. Kirk is adamant that

'Very few people know or acknowledge that *The Woman in Black* was to be a motion picture and filmed on 35mm. I was never sure why it reverted to a TV movie, but I suspect some executives developed cold feet'. (A report on British films currently in production, including *TWIB*, that appeared in industry publication *Screen International* on 4 February 1989 supports the fact that it was at that point intentioned as a feature film.) These cold feet cost time and resources, and had the potential to compromise the creative integrity of the project, which lost two weeks of its schedule and the deployment of cinematic technology. But as will be discussed throughout the following chapters, *TWIB* is a creatively ambitious work, and Wise continued undaunted by behind-the-scenes changes.

Importantly, he also had the capacity to inspire his team to carry on with him, and Kirk vividly recalls the impact of Wise's determination: 'when the heads of department were told of the change in scheduling and the financial restrictions that were to be put in place, all, without exception, chose to stay on board. This was mainly because Mr Wise was to be the Director'. Kirk felt he developed an extraordinarily effective working relationship with Wise, and still speaks of him in terms of the highest respect: 'I had worked with Mr Wise before, and we quickly developed an almost symbiotic relationship. How or why this came about, to this day, I have yet to learn'. However, there may be clear reasons. Kirk recollects a director who made explicit what he wanted, who planned meticulously (always a bonus for a first assistant whose job it is to keep the production on track), and who was also open to good ideas and would graciously give credit where credit was due:

> As he once said to me and no doubt countless others: 'Tell me your ideas. If they are good, I will use them and take the credit'. It was his way of saying let's do the best we can with whomever we can. In this way, people always felt they could go to him with suggestions or ideas, whether he adopted them or not. If he accepted the contributor's ideas, he would thank them sincerely, telling all and sundry from whom the idea came.

Above we described *TWIB* as a labour of love and one story from Kirk's memories shows the unusual level of personal commitment people felt towards making this work as special as possible, to the extent they were prepared to pay from their own pockets to ensure the ending had something special. The story of this commitment merits telling in full in Kirk's own words:

> in the final sequence with the last apparition of the Woman at the lake (Underwater Tower with access by boat to poor freezing Pauline), Mr Wise decided we needed a camera crane to emulate the falling tree on Arthur and his family. It was to be a Chapman Titan. We were told that the film could not afford it. By this time, we were all completely exhausted and wanted the film to finish on a dramatic high. The culmination of six-day weeks and sometimes fifteen-hour days led me to say to the Grip Company that I would pay for the crane and the technicians. I did this privately. It was not until the day of filming when the key grip came to me asking if I was paying his wages did Mr Wise realise how the crane came to be there. So, he said he would contribute as well. We both wrote out cheques, as indeed did some other crew members. Finally, the company relented and never cashed the cheques, but we had our shot and film.

Chapter Two: 'Vying with one another to tell the horridist, most spine-chilling tale': Authorship and Adaptation

This chapter examines the creative adaptive processes of turning a pseudo-period novella into a television film, examining the key creative players in turn: the writer of the book, its adaptor, and the director. As signalled in the introduction, Kneale did not hesitate to make changes he thought necessary. His actions point to the emphasis in this chapter on the competition for authorial control between the text in question and its competing iterations in written, theatrical, and cinematic form, situating the 1989 film as the focus among a sequence of other iterations of the story. We argue, first, that part of its 'horror' as film emanates from *TWIB*'s liminal status and, as Kim Newman stated, as a text that echoes a haunting itself – via a compulsion to repeatedly return to the work, in this case a source novella (DVD commentary, 2020). Concomitantly, we will consider *TWIB* as a text, in its competing iterations, which exemplifies an understanding of horror, or the gothic horror in particular, as post-modern in its capacity to 'resurrect' in different forms on both film and television (Punter, 2001). Secondly, this chapter will address the specific adaptation of the text itself, as a powerful aesthetic marker in presenting its own version of the story, navigating the interstitial vacuum between novel, television, and cinematic text owing to the impact of these various creators. The argument that this is a cinematic work of horror will be established here through close examination of its aesthetic qualities and its authorial shaping.

In pursuit of these aims, we consider the creative interplay of multiple authors and multiple interpretations of the source text, a process reflecting the opening of the original novella and the competition among the film's key stakeholders to create a 'version' of the text and to tell their own story. This will be positioned in the creative context of the preceding theatre version, novel, and then the later film, each showing differing aesthetic approaches that are revealing of the strengths and diversities of opposing/complementary media. Central to this study will be a consideration of authorship, and the numerous forces shaping this process. We study the book's author, Susan Hill, and her canon of work and her own influences, including the Edwardian scholar and bibliographer M. R.

James and, by extension, James's own influence on haunted television adaptations through the 'ghost stories for Christmas' of 1970s television.

However, as Kim Newman asserted, the 1989 version of the text is primarily 'remembered as a work by Nigel Kneale' (DVD commentary, 2020). Thus, the chapter will consider the major additions made by Nigel Kneale, and in relation to his authorial canon in the realms of horror, fantasy, and science fiction brought from cinema to television. Kneale's most significant changes/contributions include name changes from the novella and use of local dialect, as well as a major change to the ending: in the novella and play, use of first-person narration suggests the survival of the main protagonist, yet Kneale had licence to create an even greater/heightened catastrophe to a cinematic scale.

The chapter will consider the authorial contribution of director Herbert Wise, his other work, and his noted ability to elicit specific performances from actors. As an 'auteur' himself, Wise is underappreciated – something this book will seek to redress.

These stakeholders will be considered in the context of TV technology and aesthetics as they were by 1989 – including Kneale and his writing style and structure for his BBC works, as opposed to writing for the different dynamic expectations of commercial television needing advertisement breaks, an ability most powerfully expressed by the pre-ad 'screeching woman' in the bed manifestation scene. As such, and as this chapter will argue, the film is viewed in or out of context depending on how it is viewed. A film 'made for TV' or 'a TV film' offer a subtle but nonetheless important distinction in understanding the formal and material processes at play in producing and disseminating horror.

Creative context: ghosts at Christmas

British television audiences expect to be frightened at Christmas. British readers have even older expectations and in addition to writing his own ghost stories, the antiquarian and writer M. R. James found in manuscript and published ghost stories dating from the Middle Ages (James, 1922: 413–22; Simpson, 2003: 394). Ghosts, including those of vengeful women, recur in English folklore (Handley, 2015: 242). Charles Dickens made noteworthy contributions in the Victorian period. Hill's novella begins with a family telling ghost stories, the homely domesticity undercut by the protagonist's traumatic memories of seeing a ghost for real. By the 1970s, the oral and literary traditions of telling ghost stories were well established via books and on television, including Kneale's own *The Stone Tape*. Eerie children, haunted houses, frightened governesses, and other tropes were both cinematic and television commonplaces. Before considering in more detail what Hill wrote, what Kneale changed in adaptation, and how Herbert Wise brought the story onto the screen as director, studying the wider creative context will shed useful light on 1989's ghostly broadcast.

While certain themes and characteristics recur across her works, Hill's 1983 novella connects beyond these to a longer set of themes and styles in English ghost stories, reworking what Val Scullion refers to as the 'conventional Gothic tropes such as the haunted rooms, old manuscripts and a naive narrator' (2003: 295). To these could be added the haunting presence of children. These connections transpose to the 1989 adaptation. Where critics and readers have noted the stylistic and thematic links between the novella and the written works of M. R. James, the television adaptation as a piece of period drama broadcast at Christmas time connects through association with the *A Ghost Story for Christmas* strand made by the BBC, primarily from M. R. James's stories. The drama strand began with *The Stalls of Barchester* in 1971, adapted from 'The Stalls of Barchester Cathedral' published in 1910's *More Ghost Stories of an Antiquary*. The following four stories in successive years were all James's – *A Warning to the Curious*, *Lost Hearts*, *The Treasure of Abbot Thomas*, and *The Ash Tree* – followed by Charles Dickens' *The Signalman* and then two modern and original stories, *Stigma* and *The Ice House*.

These established and consolidated an eagerly anticipated tradition, based on the frisson of pleasure that comes from a ghost story told in a cold, dark English Christmas. That same ghost-story-telling tradition is evoked at the start of Hill's novella when Kipps' stepchildren unwittingly traumatise him by telling ghost stories around the fire. For 1970s television audiences, however, there was great pleasure to be had from the BBC's wintry ghost stories. Punctuating the BBC's Christmas broadcasts for over a decade, and gaining tonal coherence from Lawrence Gordon Clarke's direction and production on location on 16mm films, the drama strand was conspicuously successful.

The 11-year gap between the BBC's *The Ice House* and *TWIB* served merely to highlight the well-remembered recent tradition of a ghost story for Christmas Eve, mostly in a period setting. By the time of *TWIB*'s broadcast in 1989, trade papers, television writers, and the television listings all took it as axiomatic that there would be a ghost story on television for Christmas (see the introduction).

While the BBC's *A Ghost Story for Christmas* drama strand is an immediately compelling context for *TWIB*, and had informed expectations about ghost stories on Christmas Eve television, the relationships between the strand and *TWIB* is complex. As works made on 16mm film and mostly in period settings, the BBC's stories are stylistic and technical forerunners for the location filming on *TWIB*. As discussed later, this mode of production was wholly different from how Herbert Wise made other acclaimed works in his career. In *I, Claudius* the multi-camera electronic recording in a BBC studio meant the actors performed whole scenes almost as though under a proscenium arch. On film, each shot has its own set up. Each scene is constructed from the shots.

Even the approach of the actors to their acting is different from videotape to film. Compared to recording in an electronic studio, where whole scenes are rehearsed and then recorded in totality, actors on film give a piecemeal performance, shot by shot. As also discussed later in this chapter, Wise seamlessly and with great versatility transitioned from the in-house videotape production of the 1970s to his stylish film work in 1989, but the glossier and location-made work on *TWIB* instantly evokes the influence of the BBC's ghost stories.

The production of *TWIB* picks up the Jamesian cues in the bulk of the BBC adaptations. While these influences in part are directly from James to Hill, Kneale himself was influenced by James and contributed an introduction to an edited selection of James's ghost stories in 1973. The ecclesiastical settings in the church and around the ruined abbey and graveyard echo many settings in James's stories and the bleak and damp East Anglian setting evokes James also. These are influences on Hill but also on Kneale. In other works such as *Quatermass and the Pit* Kneale used ecclesiastical settings and what Cottis (2024) calls 'clerical antiquarians' inspired by characters in James's stories. In the novella Hill makes explicit her emulation of James and the chapter titled 'Whistle and I'll Come to You' evokes the title of James's short story 'Oh, Whistle, and I'll Come to You, My Lad', published in *Ghost Stories of an Antiquary* in 1904. In 1968 Jonathan Miller directed an adaptation for the BBC with the title reduced to *Whistle and I'll Come to You*, establishing a naming pattern then used in Hill's novella as an 'atavistic acknowledgment of the supernatural tale' (Cook, 2014: 150). In writing *TWIB*, a potent creative framework of mutually reinforcing literary, film, and television works surrounded Hill. While the tropes mentioned above of haunted rooms, old manuscripts, and a naive narrator are rather staid, they are sharpened by the influence of another theme, what Michael Cook aptly summarises as 'the death of children and the appalling consequences which flow from it' (2014: 146).

The multiple layers of tragedy in the novella, including the death of Kipps' wife and child, the deaths of other children in the local town, and even the nihilistic lethargy and ennui which have gripped the adults in the town as they live under the shadow of supernatural terrors (such as a local businessman Sam Daily buying up land simply for something to do) all stem from the death of the woman's child on the marshes. Haunting of and by children informed Henry James's 1898 novella *The Turn of the Screw*, turned into a successful and influential film, *The Innocents*, in 1961. Ghostly children also appeared in M. R. James's 'Lost Hearts', a short story published in 1905. ('Lost Hearts' became an instalment of the BBC's ghost stories for Christmas in the 1970s.) This story takes in many ways a different path to Hill's. In 'Lost Hearts' two children have been murdered, their hearts being removed, and now their spirits haunt the house where they met their grisly demise. In contrast, the catalyst for the haunting in the 1983 novella was a tragic accident on the causeway rather than a deliberate murder. But as Cook points out, both stories feature 'an intensely personal encounter with a ghost', the encounter in both instances with a naive narrator (2014: 155).

In what follows, the way Kneale adapted the text will be described in more detail, but while making changes he was mostly faithful to the story. He also had a lot of content to work with as he was scripting from a novella, not a short story. It is actually odd that M. R. James's ghost stories have such a longstanding history of television adaptation, as they are virtually unfilmable. By that is meant that they are all short stories, some no more than a few pages, with scarcely enough action to sustain even half an hour of television. Much of the pleasure of his works also lies in their literary qualities that cannot be easily translated to screen. Among his many scholarly accomplishments, James could pastiche assorted styles of historical text, from a seventeenth-century law report in 'Martin's Close' to writing his own mediaeval-style

Latin or pastiches of Anglo-Saxon riddles (Murphy, 2018: 99). These features do not provide filmable content, meaning that adaptors of this work, not only in the BBC's versions but also in *Mystery and Imagination* and even NBC's 1961 adaptation *Room 13*, must deviate from the source text, often drastically.

Adaptation

So how faithful an adaptation is *TWIB*? Adaptation, especially turning a book into a script for a film or television production, is cogently and critically analysed in Linda Hutcheon's *A Theory of Adaptation* (2006). Scrutinising a process which will adapt, adjust, alter, or make suitable, Hutcheon finds that adaptation overall is a process of repetition 'without replication' from the original work. Before Kneale set to work to adapt the novella into a screenplay, the playwright Stephen Mallatratt had already dramatically transformed the story into a successful theatre version. Mallatratt jettisoned all the supporting characters and rendered down the story to a two-man play, with a brief appearance also by the 'woman'. In the unconventional retelling of the story, the character of Kipps yields to a character of a professional actor on stage to tell the story of his encounter with a ghost, with just two performances ultimately portraying a host of different characters. Mallatratt's play premiered in 1987 and was both an instant and enduring success, being easy to stage, having only two lead parts, and designed to be performed with minimalist sets and few props. Trade paper *The Stage* gave it a glowing review as a 'masterpiece' that had been 'brilliantly adapted' and performed by actors who 'give superb performances in their catalogue of roles which dissolve into a splendid array of characters' (7 January 1988: 10).

The 1989 television film is more faithful to the novella than the 2012 Hammer film or the 1987 play. It follows a linear narrative taking place in the present moment. However, from beginning to end, Kneale intrudes his own authorial intentions to make changes that range from the mild to the drastic. He follows all of Hill's plot fundamentals. A senior lawyer sends a young lawyer to the remote Eel Marsh House, a place isolated from the nearby town except when the causeway appears. He attends the funeral of their client Mrs Drablow and begins to organise the late woman's legal and official paperwork. While there he befriends a rich local landowner, spends a terrifying night at the cues in the novella that this older man had suffered, and the script describes 'a man of 50. His hair is completely white. His face is pale and prematurely lined. He has undergone a great deal of stress in his life, and it shows'. Kneale's descriptions of the clothing and 'a 1950-style telephone' set the period long after the Edwardian era. In further description, Kneale was at pains that the set design would show what makeup, casting, and dialogue would also convey and he instructed that

> The room is remarkably bare. Nothing can have been done to it for years. There is cracked brown paint on the cupboards and cabinets. The walls are almost peeling. The leather chairs are scuffed white. In fact, apart from a couple of bad formal oil paintings of former partners, there is nothing at all personal here. It is as if he inhabits it, and works in it, without ever having attempted to make it his own.

Although he has moved the opening's setting from a Christmas fireside to a place of business, Kneale has initially preserved intact from the novella an older but defeated and traumatised Kidd who had lived to tell a tale. The ending of the first draft was mostly faithful to the novella; but Kneale also showed from the first draft that his use of the book would be subject to his own creative interpolations. In the novella, Kipps' wife and child die in a riding accident, and initially the draft looks as though it will follow this plotting, for as described by Kneale, a sudden intrusion of sound and confusion was to take place: 'Suddenly… the sound of hooves. Clip-clop… Clip-clop' and 'For an appalling moment ARTHUR cannot place the source of it. Just as it was on the causeway. He looks wildly around, only half expecting to see anything'. But here Kneale both adapts and subverts. In the novella the woman steps out, scares the horses and in the confusion Mrs Kipps and the child die. Kneale though was originally planning something else, for the horses 'go trotting calmly away'. Here Kneale may be writing for the benefit of people familiar with the novella, who would have known there was a riding accident, and his scene plays with this prior knowledge and then adds an extra shock, for the horses do not kill but the water does.

In the next scene a tree falls and sinks the boat. Stella and the baby die but Arthur does not. Instead, Kneale describes a scene of underwater corpses that would have been gruesome if realised on screen: 'He finds his family. STELLA, still clutching baby but crushed and dead, with open eyes. And then EDDIE, floating deep and trapped…'

(105). Then follows a short final scene, a reprise to where the action started in the 1950s and suggestive of Hill's original story with Kidd marrying again and becoming a stepfather. Even this first draft, though, uses but changes the original, for whereas in the novella the later action showed Kipps remarried and part of his new family, the first draft ends on a far more ambiguous note with Kidd 'weighed down by ancient horrors' and the script ends when he 'tries to give them a welcoming smile…' (106).

The ending in the first draft is more or less what appeared in the final draft, with the critical difference that by the second draft (then unchanged in the third) Kidd also drowns, so the 1950s coda vanishes. But from the first draft Kneale had already decided on the way the woman would make her final apparition when Kidd 'sees the impossible. It is the WOMAN. Standing twenty feet behind them, on the surface of the water' (105). The description is identical in the third version, except that Kneale has used the typewriter to underline the words 'on the surface of the water' (103) as though to ensure the director realises he will need to depict something uncannily impossible.

The vivid and detailed descriptions of the weary man of the 1950s and his drab environment offer an equally vivid and intriguing insight into Kneale's imagination and process of world building. As other papers in the Isle of Man Archives reveal, including the variety of drafts for what became the 1979 *The Quatermass Conclusion*, Kneale imagined himself deeply into his stories and their worlds. In notes written mostly for his own benefit, he worked out how the dystopian state of affairs in Britain had come to pass. Kneale entered in depth to creating the world and its people. The second draft of the script included Kneale's list of characters with ages given for each. The third draft also includes his own potted biographies for the major characters. Mostly these are consistent with the points in the novella although Kneale has given each character an exact age and date of birth. Significantly, he has also given Eel Marsh House itself a short biography and these points are departures from the novel. According to the notes, it was 'Built in 1884 by Morgan Drablow, before his marriage to Alice. Electric lighting system installed in 1894. Dictaphone installed 1900'. As discussed later, the electrification of the house and the recording technology are important additions brought in from Kneale's imagination.

But to return to the weary, 50-year-old Kidd, this opening shows Kneale as originally far more indebted to the novella than the finished version. In short, Kidd lives to tell the tale. Other changes show the progress of his thinking. While Kidd survives in Kneale's first version, the first draft included a graphically described sequence in which the small gypsy girl does not. In the final version as filmed, Kidd pulls her free in time before logs on a lorry crush her. But in the first draft, 'ARTHUR crouches over the CHILD's body. It is horribly, hopelessly crushed'. The gory description may have given makeup and special effects a field day in depicting a crushed child but may also have pushed the boundaries of what was acceptable for broadcast; in the last version, the deaths of Nathaniel Drablow and Edmund Toovey have occurred off screen, recounted in later narrative, and the camera cuts away from showing the Kidd family being crushed by the tree falling on their boat. The difference shows Kneale changing his mind on who lives and who dies. But the interplay of the living and the dead across the first, second, and third drafts is noteworthy. In dialogue in the first draft, immediately after the girl is crushed to death, the shocked Arthur mumbles 'She might have been at the school. I saw them there. By the church. They were watching. The funeral'. The dialogue refers back to an earlier scene, when Kidd had seen children watching over the fence of the churchyard, where Kidd had already noticed a large number of children were buried.

The church and churchyard are the location of one other significant planned scene which Kneale drafted, edited in the next draft, and then ultimately omitted. In the filmed version the vicar, although played by the notable character actor John Franklyn-Robbins, is a minor character seen only intoning the funeral service. In the first and second drafts, he plays a more significant part as Kidd returns to the church seeking both information and spiritual comfort from the vicar, explaining to him that he sensed 'something bad', 'what you would probably call… evil' in the church. But as scripted, the Reverend Mr Greet responds with indignation. 'How dare you come in here and start talking about superstition! In my church!', adding 'I've fought this for years. [Kneale has added "Round here" in pencil.] They'll believe in anything, any kind of spooky nonsense to frighten themselves with! And you've caught it!' The vicar's anger would have made the character stand out from all other local inhabitants, from Toovey to the local farmers, who are all gripped with a fatalistic ennui and despair. This brief and explosive exchange, coming at about half way through the script, would also have been a moment of passion and energy raising the action briefly before the sequences of Kidd alone at

Table 1. Main changes from novella to film

Hill	Kneale
Character names and identities	
Kipps	Kidd
Sam Daily	Sam Toovey
Jennet Eliza Humfrye	Janet Goss
Character relationships	
Kipps enters partnership with employer	Kidd sacked by employer
Marital status	
Kipps has fiancée	Kidd has wife and children
Beginning	
Kipps with new family	Kidd with original family
Ending	
Kipps sees wife and child die	Kidd and his family all die
Wife and child die in accident with horses	The family drowns when tree falls on boat
Kipps has wife and stepchildren	Kidd has died
Storytelling	
First-person narrative	Objective narrative
Structure	
Story as flashback	Linear narrative

Eel Marsh House. However, by the final draft Kneale dropped the scene. The vicar's desperately defiant rejection of ghosts and superstition disappears, leaving a more consistent storytelling texture of an entire community alert to the woman in black who has been killing their children. Interestingly, another addition by Kneale dropped from the final version is the voice of Mrs Drablow on the wax discs affirming that, far from purely haunting her, the ghost affirms her faith, while the vicar struggles with his. (Toovey suggests that the vicar is a 'fool' who 'has trouble believing in God' in Kneale's early draft.) Mrs Drablow asserts that the apparition 'brings me comfort – I can now believe there is no death'.

Elsewhere, it is suggested that the name changes in Kneale's adaptations are a way of him finding an entry point and personal attachment to the work of another writer (Newman, DVD commentary 2020). Another point of admiration is the 'sheer economy' and timbre of Kneale's dialogue, which creates 'perfect', 'thumbnail sketches' (Nyman and Gatiss, DVD commentary 2020). Especially singled out for praise by Mark Gatiss and others in the DVD commentary is the dialogue given to Sam Toovey, the first instance of which occurs in an exchange with Arthur on the train:

>Arthur – 'I expect to be in and out of there [Eel Marsh House] for several days'.
>
>Sam – 'Do you now?'

The grim foreboding is expressed through Sam's dialogue and actor Bernard Hepton's delivery – part of the subtle 'slow-burn' of the adaptation. Another scene with Sam, in which he talks listlessly with his wife and Arthur at the dinner table, uses economy and suggestion to indicate a shared trauma between the couple, in which the loss of a child is implicated through the ceaseless attempt to fill the void through work:

>Sam – 'Why do I do it?'
>
>Arthur – 'I don't know – why do you?'
>
>Sam – 'I don't know. No reason except to go on and on. Doing it becomes its own reason you see. And in the end, there's no point at all. It's like all hobbies, essentially pointless.

[to Mrs Toovey]

'Do you agree Margaret? My territorial ambitions are singularly pointless?'

At this point, Mrs Toovey, visibly upset, retires from the dinner table.

Kneale builds on the original in other ways. Most notably, after Kipps has his terrifying night at Eel Marsh House, he attempts to rest and sleep at the nearby inn. In the novella, Hill notes that in his disturbed state, he sensed the woman in black at the foot of his bed. Kneale, however, turns that single line into the explosively frightening apparition of the woman, creating as he did so the best-remembered part of the whole film. In other ways Kneale amplifies or draws out the potential of the novella. In the book, Mrs Drablow is dead by the time the action commences and is an unseen, voiceless aspect of the story, her character and personality only apparent from the mute paperwork and the impression made by her rather mundane household effects. Kneale gives the character posthumous voice. Clearly Kneale found inspiration in Hill's novella, but also did not hesitate to make changes he thought would ease its transition into a script. Both Hill and Kneale were and remain acclaimed writers and now is time to consider both in more detail.

ADAPTATION: THE NOVELIST

Kneale made changes to a well-received novella that itself drew on and adapted from other writers and their themes. Susan Hill's writing career was precocious and began at university with the publication of *The Enclosure* in 1961. By 1983 she had authored a further eight novels. Some common themes or characteristics appear in these that shaped *TWIB*, from the bleak coastal settings (*A Change for the Better*, 1969; *The Albatross*, 1971), unsettling old houses (*I'm the King of the Castle*, 1970), historical settings around the end of the nineteenth and into the early twentieth centuries (*Strange Meeting*, 1971), and madness (*The Bird of Night*, 1972). Since the 1990s her work has continued in similar veins, using period settings in *From the Heart* (2017), isolated houses in *The Beacon* (2008), and subverting the innocence of children and children's toys by imbuing them with menace in *The Small Hand* (2010) and *Dolly: A Ghost Story* (2012). In 2007 she published *The Man in the Picture: A Ghost Story* and in

2016 she published *The Travelling Bag and Other Ghostly Stories*, returning again to the supernatural themes of *TWIB*.

TWIB novella is a pastiche but that is not to say it is derivative nor that all of its inspirations are immediately obvious. Careful study of key themes and even detailed study of phrasing suggests unusual and obscure sources of inspiration for Hill that in turn provided creative cues for Kneale to follow. Although sometimes called neo-Victorian (Burkhard, 2016), Hill's novella takes place in the twentieth century, in a world with motor cars and electricity but also where travel by horse and carriage is still typical. In that regard its setting is somewhat interstitial, as the modernity of the twentieth century is apparent but links to the nineteenth century are also present.

The woman herself is one of those links from the Victorian past to the twentieth-century present day. Her malevolent and leering apparitions are in fact an intrusion of the Victorian period into the twentieth century. As a revenant, the woman remains frozen in the style and appearance of her own time and appears to people as a ghost in the clothing and style of the previous century, as described by Hill and visualised on screen by the costume design. Hill's novella therefore depicts not only a Victorian ghost but the Victorian morality and attitudes which blasted the woman's happiness as still intruding in the twentieth century. The woman's backstory is her conceiving a child out of wedlock, condemning her to the perdition of a fallen woman and social outcast, whose tragedy is worsened when the son she had given up for adoption dies in an accident on the causeway.

This spectral but angry Victorian woman suggests another source Hill drew from. Where the stories of M. R. James are mostly Edwardian in setting, they are also masculine, deriving from stories James told in all-male school and collegiate settings, and normally about men. The woman in black though is a malevolent and violent intrusion of Victorian femininity. As Burkhard points out, the woman does not get to tell her story and has no voice in the narrative. Kneale follows this point and apart from some screeching noises, the woman emits no sound. Kipps/Kidd instead tells her story, as he painstakingly reconstructs it from documents, photographs, sound recordings, and the meaning he accords to the sonic and visual apparitions which torment him. But while a man tells her story for her, the woman is a force of female hatred and agency far removed from the masculine storytelling which prevails in James's ghost stories.

While readers and scholars compare Hill to James, a more meaningful but overlooked comparison is with the ghost stories written by Lettice Galbraith. Galbraith's life and writing career are shrouded in obscurity, including until recently basic facts such as the exact dates of her birth and death. She is known, however, for her late-Victorian supernatural stories, collected as *New Ghost Stories* in 1893. These are authentic Victorian ghost stories rather than neo-Victorian pastiche and she ranks alongside other female writers of ghost stories with psychological themes and manifestations of evil female ghosts. Galbraith's stories are from a period when literary genres were porous. As Melissa Edmundson (2017) points out, what modern readers and scholars may call simply ghost stories were also considered 'weird stories' by their contemporary readers and the unstable generic descriptions are partly because of the way women writers were crafting stories which were so inherently peculiar, they defied stable generic definition.

As a writer of a period-style pastiche, Hill is an inheritor of this generic adventurousness, but also as a writer of a pastiche she copies from the lively and peculiar works of the nineteenth century without further pushing at generic boundaries. What Hill inherited from Galbraith is a middle-class world interrupted by spirits and other signs of the supernatural. As Liggins notes, domains such as the séance and the hypnotism chamber were particular sites of female spiritual authority (2022: 181). That authority could be destructive and vengeful. Galbraith's fiction further proposes a world where women could be both vulnerable but powerful. Both living and dead, the woman in black in Hill's story is an outcast and an outsider. In the story Kipps/Kidd reconstructs, she was born into a middle-class world which banished her because of her pregnancy when unmarried. As a ghost, she remains an outsider to society. She is an intruder from another time, as indicated by her antique clothing, and while she has power of life and death, the locals try their hardest to ignore her and pretend she does not exist.

As an outcast in both states of existence, the descriptions of the woman in Hill's novella are strikingly similar to how Galbraith had described a sexually disgraced and socially outcast woman in her short story 'In the Seance Room'. In Hill's novella, when Kipps first sees the woman (not knowing at that point she is a revenant and assuming she is simply another mourner at Mrs Drablow's funeral) he first notes her old-fashioned mourning dress. Initially, therefore, she seems to be a ghost who can 'pass for the living', a point made about spectral figures in the writings of another female author, Violet Hunt. Then,

> even the swift glance I took of the woman showed me enough to recognise that she was suffering from some terrible wasting disease, for not only was she extremely pale, even more than a contrast with the blackness of her garments could account for, but the skin and, it seemed, only the thinnest layer of flesh was tautly stretched and strained across her bones, so that it gleamed with a curious blue-white sheen.

He believes she must be suffering from a condition causing 'terrible wasting' and 'ravages of the flesh'. In Galbraith's 'In the Seance Room', the spurned and socially outcast woman appears to observers as 'a wreck of womanhood', who looks 'practically dead' and 'a spoiled ruined thing' who 'had all the appearance of a dead body' (Liggins, 2022: 182). Both women have been seduced only to experience social ruination and to lose any place in respectable society. Galbraith's stories, including 'In the Seance Room' and 'The Missing Model', feature female ghosts who are a 'vengeful revenant' and expose 'hidden secrets, regret, and repressed guilt'. The comparison is striking, again re-orienting us away from the masculine world of M. R. James towards the influences on Hill of earlier and female-authored works.

In tracing the sources of adaptation and the processes of adaptation from Hill to Kneale, factoring in the generically unstable weird stories of female writers shows a complex interplay between the nineteenth-century works, Hill's novella, and Kneale's script. The potent malignancy of a female revenant recurs from Galbraith to Hill. Hill, however, eschews many other significant themes in the weird stories of the nineteenth century. In the novella, Kipps does not need any intermediating agent such as a Ouija board, séance, or medium to summon up the aural or visual hauntings. They simply occur whether he wants them to or not, without any direction from him or a medium. Galbraith's ghosts and revenants by contrast showed the creative inspiration provided by the Theosophical Society, founded in Galbraith's lifetime. Titles of her short stories such as 'In the Seance Room' indicate the impact of spiritualism and spirit contact on her fiction.

As noted, Hill omitted any such element from her story. Kneale, however, proved alert to the uncanny properties of early technology. As noted by Emma Liggins in her study of Galbraith's fiction, the spirit contact which the Theosophical Society studied and claimed to have achieved was 'often aligned at this time with other communication forms such as telegraphy and the telephone' (2022: 180). The language of spiritualism also evoked the language of electrical technology, for example the terms 'magnetism' and 'current'. Where Hill emulates the vengeful female from late-Victorian fiction, Kneale instated the capacity for technology to seem as eerie as a séance or a hypnotism chamber. Kneale's script inserts into the story (as discussed elsewhere in our study) the 'new-fangled' technologies installed at Eel Marsh House. Through the medium of the wax discs and the dictaphone, the late Mrs Drablow is able to speak from beyond the grave just as if speaking via a séance. Kneale elegantly and logically extends what was original in the novella and the aural haunting of the accident on the causeway described by Hill and brought onto the screen is itself a type of recording, now paralleled through Kneale's addition with the actual recordings on the wax cylinders. What initially seems to Kidd to be an amusing novelty is soon revealed to be part of a sinister narrative.

There is a compelling ghostly precedent for Kneale's changes. As Sean O'Connor points out, the arguably most-famous haunted house in Britain, Borley Rectory in Essex, was haunted via technology. Interestingly, the story of Borley Rectory's hauntings is yet to receive adequate creative adaptation. *TWIB*, a story about a haunted house in Essex, is in fact a vastly better iteration of the general contours of this story, and the reports of the hauntings at Borley Rectory are an obvious reference point for Kneale's adaptation of the story from the written word to sound and image. As O'Connor's recent work on the Borley hauntings shows, the purported ghosts at the rectory (including even a woman in black, as one of the ghosts was a nun in her habit) were actually ghosts at the cutting edge of technology. The supernatural world of the early twentieth century was one alive with the sounds of technology and electricity. As he says,

> science had identified unseen forces such as cathode rays and electromagnetic waves…. The electrical telegraph had transformed world communications, but it had also changed prevailing attitudes to communication with the dead. The imaginative

distance from the dots and dashes of Samuel Morse's code in 1837 to communicating with spirits through a system of raps… was a step rather than a leap. (2022: 116)

Unseen forces perhaps but not unheard, therefore. The hauntings at Borley were noisy, with household objects thrown around and furniture overturned, and Kneale similarly adapted the story by adding the sound of the supernatural.

In adapting the story, Kneale therefore judiciously adds to it and one of the key additions he makes is this use of sound, in among other ways through these wax cylinders. What the audience hears directly changes the nature of gendered interactions in the story. While Hill's novella told the story as a first-person narrative by Kipps, Kneale's script presents the story objectively. There is no privileged authorial voice, merely the scrutiny of the objective camera. One dramatic possibility would have been to have Kidd's voice heard over the top of the action as a voiceover. However, Kneale's drastic change to the ending, so that not only the wife and child but Kidd himself die would have made that a narrative absurdity. Instead, in Kneale's adaptation Kidd loses his authorial or narrative voice entirely. The woman may not get to speak, but Kidd does not get to tell his own story. In the novella, that had at least been his one remaining source of power over the woman in black: he lived to tell the tale and what we know of her, we know from Kipps' words. Studying Kipps' first-person narrative in the novella, Scullion notes that while Kipps retains the position as first-person narrator throughout the whole story, he loses authority to the woman. Drawing on Gina Wisker's notion of radical women's horror, 'which undermines patriarchal tendencies to define and confine women' (Scullion, 2003: 296), Scullion suggests that despite retaining undisputed his position as the storyteller, the woman weakens Kipps.

However, that point could be taken too far. As noted, all we know of the woman is from Kipps' authorial descriptions, including his pitilessly detailed physical descriptions of her ravaged appearance, an objectification of her which surely confines and defines her. Far from losing his authority, it is suggested his storytelling may even be empowering and cathartic. Stricken at the start of the novella when his stepchildren all demand he tell a ghost story, Kipps essentially 'mans up' and tells the story of the woman in black to conquer his fears. Kneale though is more radical. Kneale robs the character of his authorial voice and then even his life. When we hear Kidd's voice either live or on a wax recording, he is speaking into someone else's drama. In Kneale's script, one of the first and most significant changes is to what we hear, in that we are not allowed to hear Kidd's thoughts.

In other ways, Kneale added sound throughout the story and his script intrudes sounds from multiple sources. The story is remarkably noisy, and where we lose as viewers the first-person narrative we had as readers, we gain an often-startling soundscape in its place. Sounds of all types abound, with cheerful giving way to sinister. In an early scene Kidd's son is joyously playing with his duck caller and the family all enjoy the happy and raucous sounds. Kidd himself has some musical talent and can hold a tune. Perhaps the most notable addition to the story's soundscape is the participation of the apparatus for sound recording in the storytelling and the sonic texture of the film. In the novella, Mrs Drablow's affairs were left to posterity in silent piles of dusty documents. These written records are also in the screen version, but so too is her dictaphone.

From the vantage of viewers in 1989, the Edison dictaphone apparatus was an antique, but within the diegesis it is part of the Drablows' interest in 'new-fangled things', just as their electricity generator was also modern technology. Telling the story visually, Kneale's scripted directions and the performance by Adrian Rawlins shows how Kidd intuits its assembly and operation. In the script, Kneale had indicated that Kidd should show the viewers his innate understanding of the technology: 'ARTHUR lifts the cover. It is a dictaphone, an old model. With its rack of wax recording-cylinders. This is something he recognises. He turns a switch and the machine emits a faint buzz. It works!' From this visual storytelling, the use of the dictaphone is an ingenious way Kneale's script can adapt from a novella written as a first-person narrative, but avoid having a character talk to himself. Instead, Kidd talks to the dictaphone, enabling him to tell it and viewers how increasingly unnerved he becomes not by what he sees but by what he hears. The dictaphone and the generator bring their clattering, clicking, and thumping sounds into the sound design. The dictaphone not only records sound onto its wax cylinders, but makes noises as it is cranked to wind up its mechanism, and ticks and clicks when in operation in an otherwise-silent house. The heavy machinery that powers the electricity hisses and thumps when in operation. While the ghost is a revenant from the nineteenth century, the most sinister noises in the film are made by the most modern technology.

The titular woman in black has only a few moments of screen time and no dialogue. Yet Kneale's adaptation finds ways for sound to be part of the haunting. The late Mrs Drablow, unseen and unheard in the novella, adds her voice to the dialogue, and through the medium of sound she in turn speaks of the horror sound, saying to the posterity provided by the wax cylinders that 'the worst part was the noises'. Kidd adds his own voice to the eerie soundscape, using the dictaphone to record his impressions of what he has heard on the causeway. These additions take their cue from, but also enrich, the novella's descriptions of sonic hauntings.

Adaptation: the director

To turn from the script writer to the director: by 1989, the Austrian-born director Herbert Wise had been making television since 1957. By the time he made *TWIB*, he had already capped off his distinguished career by winning the 1982 Directors' Guild of America's Outstanding Directorial Achievement in Specials/Movies for TV/Actuality for *Skokie*, for which he received the Primetime Emmy nomination. His productions *I, Claudius* (1976) and *The Norman Conquests* (1977) received BAFTA nominations (the former also a Primetime Emmy nomination). Kim Newman suggested that Wise 'ought to be remembered as a major director' while Andy Nyman talks of the 'brilliance of Herbie's direction, such a brilliant actor's director… he gets these tiny moments out of people' (DVD commentary, 2020). Seen in its full perspective, Wise's career is astounding for its diversity. He was by no means a horror specialist. The diversity pertains not only to the subject matter of his television productions and occasional cinema films, but also to their production methods.

I, Claudius may reasonably be described as his masterpiece. The 13-part 1976 series based on Robert Graves' novels set in imperial Rome was showered in award nominations from the BAFTAs, the Emmys, and the Royal Society of Television for various aspects including art design, acting, and as drama. Later years have only reiterated this acclaim. Despite this, the production itself has little to distinguish it from the many drama and period series made at the BBC Television Centre in the 1970s. It was made on sets in an electronic studio recording on videotape, rather than on locations on film. The production context and technology shape the creative output.

Like productions from the 1976 adaptation of *David Copperfield*, the 1971 adaptation of *Wives and Daughters*, and the 1974 production of *The Pallisers*, not to mention series from *Dad's Army* to *Doctor Who*, shows made in the studios of Television Centre had distinctive characteristics of pacing, tone, and style.

The limitations in editing videotape gave drama a distinctive pace and the acting a degree of staginess, and the lighting was restricted by what the cameras could register. Thinking particularly of the interaction between the actors and the cameras in 1970s drama such as *Armchair Theatre*, Caughie suggests that the 'actors inhabit a space, rather than being constricted by a frame', and therefore occupy 'a space for acting – rather than a narrative space – a space for action' (2000: 77). While *I, Claudius* received acclaim on broadcast and remains highly regarded, it may be that its success lies in a number of exceptionally strong performances transcending the technical limitations of videotaped drama. Wise's direction, in contrast, is now sometimes reviewed as somewhat lacklustre. Limited as he was by the largely redundant multi-camera set up, his direction seems static in comparison to modern drama. As television writer David Stubbs (2011) notes, 'There are long, "unblinking eye" camera shots, occasionally trundling in for close-ups in moments of high drama, with very few cuts'.

But is that the case? A short detour to how Wise directed *I, Claudius* shows his versatility, or what could also be called his journeyman approach to directing. *I, Claudius* has an aesthetic compelled by the in-house production methods of the Television Centre. Yet Wise himself recalled being an agent for change in getting cameras to move more in studios. He recalled his frustration with the cumbersome movement, resulting in static shots, of the heavy cameras that had to be pushed around a studio by a four-man team when instead he wanted liveliness and mobility with the camera responding to the actor, not the other way around (cited in McNaughton, 2018: 33). That would still yield, though, a performative space created for the actors with the primacy in the studio given to what the actors were doing, rather than considerations of the framing of the shot, the editing, or the production values.

In fact, Stubbs is unfair. Former BBC cameraman Martin Kempton shared his memories with us of Wise's innovations on the studio floor of the Television Centre. Behind-the-scenes photos show the large electronic cameras looking incongruous next to actors in Roman togas, and the actors and cameras moved elegantly around each other. Far from trundling around, the camera crews adroitly moved their large machines on their pedestals, performing almost a ballet with the actors – and the movements were certainly choreographed: 'Many scenes were shot with minimal cuts, using the camera to develop around the actors to change the point of view. Of course, the blocking of the actors was essential to make this work. They too had to work hard to constantly "find" the lens' (personal communication, 1 September 2023). Unlike the film crew for *TWIB*, Wise's acknowledged masterpiece *I, Claudius* used wholly different technology and therefore required different directing and acting styles, a point Kempton noted:

> Unlike the film industry, TV cameramen (that generic term includes women of course) are expected to move the pedestal themselves. It is of course very heavy but it is very cleverly designed. The weight of the camera is hydraulically balanced, so it can be raised or lowered by holding the ring that surrounds the ped. This is relatively easy although it does involve a modest amount of strength. (Personal communication, 1 September 2023)

The immaculately framed and blocked shots in *I, Claudius*, perhaps most notably the scene when the Emperor Augustus confronts the (very long) line of men who have slept with his daughter, shows Wise making the most splendidly creative use of the 'ability to move the camera fluidly [which was] a speciality of several cameramen at TV Centre' (personal communication, 1 September 2023).

In other words, in a particular place and with particular skill sets, the camera operators were collaborating with actors to immaculately plan and control their movements, and they were performing 'a very difficult job as you can imagine. A typical move might involve a mid-shot of an actor sitting at a table, raising the ped as they stand and then crabbing across the studio floor to take them to a door. All this while keeping the shot smooth, perfectly framed and in focus' (Kempton, personal communication, 1 September 2023).

Bill Kirk, Wise's first assistant director on *TWIB*, has strong memories of Wise's working styles that reflect these points on how Wise worked well to get the best from his teams and his technologies. Kirk calls Wise 'an "actors' director"'. Actors and their rehearsal took priority. As Kirk recalls, Wise's working methods started with the actors and himself working through the scenes, and then and only then would the technicians be allowed to join. Wise

> would always rehearse the actors alone (where possible) on set with just the Script Supervisor. The crew would then be brought in and shown by Mr Wise what he had in mind. After the 'look and learn', his question would always be 'How long?' He would then sit in his chair, reading either the script or the newspaper and occasionally looking at his watch while we prepared the set-up.

This approach may explain the direction seen in *I, Claudius*, but Kirk also recollects Wise as 'a very accomplished technician who knew what he wanted to see and how he wanted to see it'. In other words, he was sensitive to directing actors to produce meaningful drama, but within a technical framework.

In other circumstances, Wise demonstrates a wholly different directorial style. By the time he directed the comedy-drama *Class Act* in 1994, he was on film with a mobile, dynamic camera and fast-paced editing. Generally, Wise was a director who did other people's work with not one but many directing styles, his choices often subordinate to the technology and production methods of particular programs and their production companies and facilities. His output included directing gigs in longstanding series such as *Van der Valk*, *Rumpole of the Bailey*, *A Touch of Frost*, *Softly, Softly: Task Force*, and *Elizabeth R*. Many of these are major productions, but they are collective properties, created by teams of different directors, writers, and producers, and often with a characteristic house style. Wise ended his career directing *The Bill*, a British police series which compelled any directorial individuality to disappear under an all-encompassing documentary-like house style.

What, therefore, is the significance of Wise in this interplay of people creating and adapting *TWIB*? The answer relates to his approach to making a film for television and to making a horror film. There were times in his directing career he was handed stand-alone and prestigious projects. One such was *The Gathering Storm*, a 1974 television movie with a budget large enough to afford Richard Burton. Another was *Skokie* in 1981, starring Danny Kaye. Although *The Gathering Storm*'s reception was marred by both Burton's erratic conduct owing to his drinking and controversy aroused when Burton attacked Winston Churchill in print, *Skokie* was a conspicuous success. Working in the United States and outside his usual British professional environment, Wise imposed a strong directorial vision on the project and elicited a rare non-comedic performance from Danny Kaye. In 1984, Wise directed the large-scale international television movie *Pope John Paul II*. Made in international locations with an enormous cast and receiving highly positive notices, the work showed that by the 1980s Wise was going from strength to strength. Jerry Roberts considers Wise brought the script for *Skokie* to life on the screen with 'a feeling of immediacy', and he worked with major stars again (Robert Mitchum and Deborah Kerr) in *Reunion at Fairborough*, a 'dazzling experience' (Roberts, 2009: 629).

Wise was not a horror specialist. The genres he worked across were as diverse as his directorial styles. Primarily directing serious drama, he also essayed work in comedy in *The Lovers!* (1973), Shakespearean drama (*Julius Caesar* in 1979), and costume drama (*Churchill's People*, 1975). Other directors from James Whale to Stanley Kubrick made horror films after working primarily in other genres.

However, a more meaningful comparison may be with another apparent journeyman director, Terence Fisher. Fisher's now much-studied career is best remembered for his horror productions starting with *The Curse of Frankenstein* in 1957. This internationally successful film led to Fisher's career as Hammer's most prolific director, with Dracula, Frankenstein, Mummy, and Wolfman films, among others (Sterritt, 2018: 739). However, his career in horror was essentially a third career after having directed films of all types since 1948 and before that being an editor. Among many B films he had made some A features as well, including co-directing *The Astonished Heart* with Antony Darnborough and (with the same co-director) *So Long at the Fair*, both in 1950 and the latter a notable success. He directed Hammer films after making *The Astonished Heart* and *So Long at the Fair*, and took on television direction. Without his sudden shift to, and his equally sudden success in, gothic horror, Fisher would scarcely be a footnote in British cinema history. As it is, he is a celebrated horror auteur but that status should not eclipse or obscure his journeyman approach to his work and the eclectic body of works which he created for film and television (Hutchings, 2001: 8).

Indeed, the notion of an alleged journeyman attempting horror should be qualified. Perceptions persist of some forms of broadcast television being inferior due to budgetary and aesthetic limitations, but also to artistic limitations, especially the notion that made-for-TV horror was not made by those steeped in the tradition of horror, but by hired journeymen. Not only was this not the case – with Steven Spielberg, Tobe Hooper, Wes Craven, and George A. Romero all contributing to televisual horror in their careers – but film directors with no track record within the genre all went on to make films now seen as part of a classic canon (James Whale – *Frankenstein*, Jack Clayton – *The Innocents*, Stanley Kubrick – *The Shining*). *TWIB* actor and *Ghost Stories* co-writer/director Andy Nyman described the expert handling of the woman manifesting on the bed sequence as 'Probably the greatest jump ever committed to film. From the sound design, the moves of every beat of this sequence just astonished me… and it's the most masterful sequence'. Of the framing and timing of the nursery sequence in which the lights go out, Nyman says that 'as a jobbing director [Wise] nails a moment that we ["experts"] would angst about' (DVD commentary, 2020). Likewise, Mark Gatiss praised the 'exquisite' production design (DVD Commentary, 2020), a point echoed by Executive Producer Ted Childs: 'I was very pleased with the quality of performance and standard of production value that Chris Burt and Herbert Wise achieved' (Murray, 2017: 266).

Wise's direction of *TWIB* has many flashes of style. A colour palette of predominantly browns and other subdued colours dominates the production design. On location and on film, rather than on videotape in a television studio, his camera can move. A long tracking shot takes the viewer across the whitewashed interior of the church during Mrs Drablow's funeral, crucially establishing its emptiness before the first apparition of the woman, but the expanse of white also creating a contrast for her dark visitation a few moments later. Whenever Kidd is climbing stairs, either at Eel Marsh House or at the local inn, the camera looks down on him from a height, therefore diminishing him in scale, making him seem vulnerable, and seeming to look over his shoulder as he moves. As Kidd has a nightmare, the camera tracks towards him, foreshadowing the screeching and remorseless movement the woman seems to make across the room as he awakes from his sleep into a further nightmare of her violently noisy apparition in the room above him. Above all, Wise's direction of the final scene, when the woman appears on a lake and the entire Kidd family die violently, is a tour de force. As violins screech, a couple of abrupt cuts towards Kidd's face create a sickening and sudden feeling of horror. Compared to the sudden movement of the cuts, the camera then stays motionless as it, the audience, and Kidd all stare at the woman. Seemingly standing on the lake, in a grotesque parody of Christ walking on the water, the woman is motionless.

Above, a comparison was drawn with Terence Fisher in terms of the journeyman director's turn to making horror films. Another comparison lies in the capacity of both Wise and Fisher to stage dynamic action with a stationary camera. In this shot, neither the woman nor the camera moves, yet the shot is alive with inexorable menace. Moving from sudden cuts to an extended pause, the stationary camera and the stationary ghost interact with one another with neither giving ground, and the woman's implacable menace permeates the scene. In other shots, Wise's static camera captures interesting shots. As the horse and cart travel across the causeway, the causeway lies across the screen looking like a coiled serpent.

Figure 2. Nine Lives Causeway with its serpentine qualities.

As this chapter argued, here are many ways to consider *TWIB* as an adaptation, beginning with its creative debt to traditions of ghost stories at Christmas that are at least as old as the Middle Ages and involve complex interplay of writers including Charles Dickens, Henry James, Lettice Galbraith, and M. R. James, the latter an influence on both Hill and Kneale. Adaptation appears in this chapter as a process involving many, from the novelist to the script writer to the director, a process illuminated by study of the different iterations of Kneale's script and the intentions of director Herbert Wise. After considering the authorial contributions of Hill and Kneale, finally, this chapter showed the contribution of Herbert Wise and his other work (including *I, Claudius*) and his noted ability to elicit specific performances from actors and strong visuals from his tools.

After this survey of the richness of the source and its adaptation, the following chapters now turn to specific themes from this richness.

Chapter Three: 'She has found a way to make me hear their calamity in the marshes': Aurality, Time, and Technology

That time and tide wait for no man is an idiom taken to its literal, logical, and terrifying extreme in *TWIB*. As suggested by Pixley, it was both the physical and aural features of the East Anglian coast that Susan Hill drew inspiration from when writing the book:

> One winter in the early 1970s, Susan borrowed a house on the Suffolk coast to use as a writing retreat for two or three months. With the property adjoining a shingle beach and facing out to sea close to the marshes, she was struck by the remoteness of the venue – the sounds of the sea, the moaning of the coastal winds, the rattling noise of the reed beds, the distant honking from a gaggle of geese. (2020: 5)

As the last chapter explored, the work of adapting *TWIB* drew on the strengths of each respective artistic and cultural form. One aspect that has remained constant is the use (or imagining) of sound as a conduit for terror. It is something evident within the original novel, and one of the principal assets of the theatrical version too. This chapter will explore further the significance of sound and technology and how they relate to notions of time and horror. Richard Hand notes that the theatrical adaptation 'is underpinned by a carefully orchestrated use of pre-recorded sound' (2014: 13) which itself drew on Hill's own consistent and evocative uses of sound (and silence). Hill describes: 'sudden, harsh, weird cries from birds' (1983: 53) and 'a sound that seemed to belong to my past, to waken old, half-forgotten memories and associations deep within me' (1983: 96). Deafening silence is evident in the following passage: 'a silence so deep, that I heard the pulsation of blood in the channels of my own ears' (1983: 46).

Even so, the sound design is one of the facets that elevate *TWIB* as a televisual film: something Mark Gatiss refers to as 'masterful' (DVD commentary, 2020). In a larger sense, televisual horror has traditionally drawn heavily on sonic properties, due in part to budgetary restrictions and in its debt to both radio broadcasts and, in the case of

Britain at least, to a long theatrical and thespian tradition. Horrific sounds can easily conjure horrific images without recourse to expensive sets, costumes, or special effects (see Fryers, 2021b).

In her analysis of gothic television, Helen Wheatley pays particular attention to the topic of sound design. Wheatley points to the 'inherent "aurality"' in *The Open Door*, one of the extant episodes of the anthology series *Mystery and Imagination*. 'Sound', Wheatley suggests, 'is not only used to imply the presence of the supernatural, but is also utilised for more routine narrative purposes' (2006: 41).

Sound in *TWIB* performs a similar function. The sounds of cars, trains, and buses in London and elsewhere, and the busy sounds of humans and cattle in Crythin Gifford, not only establish a recognisable and realistic soundscape, but subtly help to drive the narrative forward in moments of contemplation. It is a subtle use of bird noises, in particular, that helps bridge the gap between the real and the horrific in the text. The sound of blackbirds squawking at the funeral attends the woman's early appearances, creating a powerful connection between the two. Birds are also heard especially on the causeway and in the environs of Eel Marsh House, creating an atmosphere of dread and suspense (Kneale's scripts indicate the sound of curlews). Just prior to first noticing the hateful and penetrating stare of the woman in the monastery grounds, tension is subtly built up by an escalating orchestration of bird noises: oystercatchers, a carrion crow, and what is likely a black-headed gull most conspicuously build a sense of 'otherness' before the high-pitched, evocative, and uncanny noise of a curlew (repeated at other key moments of dread) fatefully signals the woman's manifestation. It works in isolation as a dread noise and a horrific leitmotif, but equally well in conjunction with Rachel Portman's musical cue, which similarly codifies and signals dread.

As argued elsewhere, sound and horror take on a special provenance within British televisual horror culture (Fryers, 2021b). Ghosts are history and British history is marked by the disembodied voices of the repressed and dispossessed – the British Isles, like Prospero's island in Shakespeare's *The Tempest*, is full of strange and disturbing noises, or as Schafer puts it, 'History is a songbook for anybody who wants to listen to it' (2005: 30).

Arthur does listen but what he hears both confuses and frightens him. After Arthur confuses the sound of the doomed pony and trap with that of Keckwick coming to deliver his safe passage from the house, his trust in his own senses never fully recovers. As Schafer suggests of auditory culture, 'We have no ear lids. We are condemned to listen' (2005: 25). Likewise, Hand asserts, 'Sound can creep and permeate like nothing else' (2014: 8).

The emphasis is also on the ability of the woman to make Alice and Arthur hear the tragedy. It is an example of her having mastery over time, space, and rationality – forcing her victims not only to see but also to hear her trauma. This is also made powerfully tangible in the inhuman screech that attends her vengeful appearance in Arthur's room.

In Chapter Two we discussed how sound was a key addition to the story when adapted by Kneale. His work is graced with the use of audio as a powerful thematic and representational means of expression. Kneale started his career in broadcasting in television's formative years, with both his *Nineteen Eighty-Four* adaptation and three *Quatermass* series being important experiments and landmark television in the 1950s. Not only did television broadcasting initially draw inspiration from its radio predecessor (the BBC held a monopoly on both until commercial broadcasting could compete from 1955), especially with regards to 'liveness', it also drew from its use of audio. This was used to carry the burden somewhat with aesthetic and budgetary limitations, although it's prudent not to overstate the case for this here, as the visual invention evident in Kneale and Cartier's *Nineteen Eighty-Four* attests (see Johnston, 2015b).

This is evident also in Kneale's works for radio. *You Must Listen* from 1952, for example, features a haunted phone line. By the 1960s, sound had become an integral part of Kneale's television works. *The Road* (1963) is a television play (sadly lost) set in 1768 in which a local squire and an Enlightenment thinker from London investigate ghostly sounds that emanate from the woods. The twist and shocking revelation is that these are not sounds from a haunted past but haunting echoes of a future world on the brink of nuclear annihilation. These were carefully crafted by Brian Hodgson of the BBC's famed Radiophonic Workshop (Murray, 2017: 121–2).

The threat of nuclear annihilation is also carried in *The Crunch*, broadcast the following year. Here, the fictional ex-colonial state of Makang threatens to detonate a nuclear bomb in a house in London. At the beginning, as chaos and tension ensue from civic and military intervention, this is brilliantly and imaginatively realised in the marked and constant sounds of traffic and car horns intruding on the speech and dialogue. In Kneale's world, the presence of unwanted sounds prefigures catastrophe on the highest scale.

Also noteworthy are Kneale's later contributions to television drama – in all instances, the intersection of time, technology, machinery, and sound points to trauma. A lost episode of the *Out of the Unknown* fantasy/horror anthology series, *The Chopper* (1971), envisaged a motorbike and its previous, deceased occupant haunting a journalist via ghostly echoes of its engine noise (a topic similarly covered in Alan Garner's *The Owl Service*, 1967 – adapted and broadcast in 1969–70). *The Stone Tape* (1972) features a group of people haunted by the ghost of a woman screaming, something they attempt to record only to uncover a far more ancient and malignant devilment.

In *During Barty's Party* (1976, part of Kneale's anthology *Beasts*) a middle-aged couple are laid siege to by a swarm of rats which are never seen, their presence indicated only by the sinister sounds they create. Likewise, in *Buddy Boy*, from the same series, the ghostly noise of the titular dolphin similarly plagues the owners of his former dolphinarium. As Abbott and Jowett suggest of *Barty's Party*, 'Kneale's emphasis upon the everyday dictated visual style, adhering to traditions of British realism by de-emphasising the gothic and the expressionist, in favour of neutral lighting and camerawork' as well as a neutral setting, as the story mostly takes place in a middle-class and ordinary living room (2013: 93). The same may be said of the aural technique: with Kneale's emphasis on the eruption of the paranatural from the quotidian taking the form of sonic expression, there is something both natural and unnatural in the rodent attack which at the end mingles with the cries of the couple.

The use of sounds is a feature of Kneale's work and often operates in connection with other recurrent themes. As Murray identifies,

> the central dramatic conflict often stems from an untamed, primal element – something from the past, from the subconscious, something buried – crashing into the present day, and playing havoc with a bright, shiny future. The present, it seems, is where the wild past, and a hopefully civilised future, collide with powerful results. (2017: 122)

Although an adaptation, the same most certainly applies in the case of *TWIB*, in which the woman is the untamed, primal element of the past, bringing chaos to the present and equally threatening, if not cancelling, the futures of Arthur, his family, and the residents of Crythin Gifford. That the haunting is carried equally in the sound of the causeway tragedy and in the woman's material presence, including her screeches, suggests the power that is embodied in aural echoes of the past.

Aside from the musical score, the sonic landscape is present even in Kneale's first draft script. From the off-screen grunting of Mr Girdler, the hissing steam and whistle of the train, the snuffling baby at the foot of the bed, and the busy sounds of the Gifford Arms and marketplace to the silence that attends the funeral directly afterwards and the 'chill little wind… whipping through the grass' when Arthur encounters the woman on the marshes, the sonic rhythms and contours are present in the writing.

Sound is heavily embedded in the detail of the script, such as at the Gifford Arms:

19. GIFFORD ARMS, NIGHT.

In the kitchen beyond there are shouts of 'Get on with it, get them pies in the oven!' … 'Done the spuds, have you?' In an exasperated WOMAN's voice. (16)

Or the market:

21. GIFFORD ARMS. DAY

The square outside is a tumult of hammering and shouting and the cries of animals, mostly cows and sheep. (19)

22. EXT GIFFORD ARMS/MARKET SQUARE. DAY.

The din hits them as they move outside. Neighing and lowing and bleating… mixed with the yells of STALLHOLDERS over their wares… From every side there are VOICES cajoling and boasting and arguing and swearing. (19)

The principal use of sound, aside from dialogue and the musical soundtrack, in *TWIB* is the sounds of Nathanial Drablow, his guardian, and Keckwick's father drowning on the marshes. Kneale's original scripts describe the event, but it is within the sound design that the full emotional and aesthetic impact is felt. Hand describes a passage of prose from Conan Doyle's *The Hound of the Baskervilles* thus: 'The passage is structured by the language of sound, making us hear and thus *feel* the environment' (2014: 15, emphasis original). The film's audio arguably functions similarly, but adding an emotional resonance that takes it to another level. Kneale's script describes it thus, with Arthur hearing the 'clip-clopping' of hooves:

> There is an appalling sequence of noises… a dreadful churning, slithering sound together with the shrill neighing and whinnying of a horse in panic. Thrashing about in glutinous mud. And human screams. (41)

It continues later:

> The Neighing has stopped, as if the unseen pony has choked to death in the quicksand. But the terrible human cries go on for a little. A kind of bubbling screams… and with it the terrified sobbing of a young child.
>
> CHILD's VOICE
>
> (almost incoherent)
>
> Mammie… Mammie….! (41)

The soundscape here is menacing – all encompassing. Along with the tide and the frets (see Chapter Four) it creates uncertainty: a monstrous intangibility. Sound, here, is a threat to the known and the rational: the basis of all horror. Arthur can shut his eyes but he can't shut his ears (although he often tries to cover them).

Music

Another distinctive feature of *TWIB* is its musical score, supplied by Academy-Award-winning composer Rachel Portman. In a stately paced drama, music as well as other audio is employed to tell the story. It establishes the contours during the fluid opening credits with a simple four-note riff that resembles a nursery rhyme (always sinister when taken out of context) with a variation, then played on flute for an otherworldly feel before converting to orchestral chords. The sinister nursery-rhyme-style tone establishes the link between children and horror which is to be a leitmotif of its own, and the escalation creates foreboding. This spare sequence lasts only a few seconds before the opening scene but creates the requisite sinister, foreboding, and expectant atmosphere, as well as suggesting associations with horror and costume drama. The musical soundtrack and its use are subtle and impactful, very much in the economical style and approach of Portman: 'I'm a big advocate for "less is more" and unfortunately there is a tendency more and more to rely on the music' (in Mackenzie, 2017).

In recent years, there has been much research into the effects, both physical and psychological, of horror music on audiences (see Hayward, 2009; Lerner, 2010; Meinel and Bullerjahn, 2022). Bernard Hermann's high-pitched, 'stabbing' string music from *Psycho* (1960) has become a mainstay of horror soundtracks (now functioning as something of a cliché) in the intervening years. Trevor, Arnal, and Frühholz suggest that horror film music, the strings in particular, 'mimics alarming acoustic feature of human screams' (2020). Here it is used to create several of these described effects.

Music also plays a part in Kneale's original scripts. In the post-coda opening of the first draft script, Arthur Kidd is described as 'whistling the hit tune of the year, 1925'. This didn't make it into the final film, but a tuneful and playful whistle that Arthur blows into the dictaphone does ('It ends with the whistle', Kneale states). They reveal a lot about Arthur's character, his gentle and playful spirit (before he is changed forever), and his attempt to assuage his disquiet with humour (also describing Mrs Drablow's personal effects as 'rubbish') following his second terrifying sighting of the woman in the grounds of the ruined abbey.

Mrs Drablow's voice also hints at the economy of the script. Her chilling lines conjure up so many potential terrors in the imagination: 'Last night she did not come until 4am. Then it was bad. A bad night'. Arthur plays this twice. Both Arthur and the audience, having by now witnessed the abject hatred burning in the woman's eyes, now imagine that she is capable of more than mere presence.

Technology and horror

Jeffrey Sconce laid out the parameters for the ongoing perception that media and technology are essentially 'haunted': 'Sound and image without material substance, the electronically mediated world of telecommunication often evokes the supernatural by creating virtual beings that appear to have no physical form' (2000: 4).

As suggested in the previous chapter, such a description could be applied to the wax disc recordings of Mrs Drablow – a voice from beyond the grave commenting on another voice and apparition from beyond the grave – a meta schemata of technology and haunting. Arthur's own recordings will join the ranks signalled by his death at the end, but the discs appear to evade destruction by fire in the first, if not the second instance. (It is also significant that Hill originally dictated the novella onto a dictaphone, as her transcriber – Jane – could not read her handwriting, and would not listen to the recordings if she was alone in the house – Pixley, 2020: 6.)

Figure 3. The wax disc recorder is an integral part of Kneale's narrative.

Michel Chion argues that sound is 'palimpsestic' (2009), which is particularly relevant to Kneale, whose work may equally be said to be the same – from the levels of history and landscape evident in *Quatermass and the Pit* and the overlapping past and present in *The Road* to the layers of history uncovered in *The Stone Tape*. Again, there are levels of time and space in non-linear alignment. It would seem that Kneale was the perfect candidate to adapt Hill's novel, therefore, as according to D'Arcy 'The Gothic genre's concern with the past's invasion of the present is exemplified in *TWIB*'s layering of "pasts" that obsessively break through and repeat/return to haunt the characters and the audience' (2022: 139).

According to Abbott and Jowett, 'In both cases [*TWIB* and *The Stone Tape*], equating the supernatural with existing technology makes the unfamiliar familiar. Kneale removes the horror from these recorded events by suggesting that they are not sentient spirits but simply echoes of past events with no tangible impact upon the present' (2013: 95). It might be added that Kneale does not necessarily remove all the horror, and the impact is very real – particularly in the case of *TWIB*. The 'familiar' and the 'unfamiliar' (or to borrow Freud's phrasing, the unheimlich) are not as binary as might be supposed – especially in the work of Kneale. The two are juxtaposed here, or at least 'layered' as D'Arcy suggests – the potential and actual eruption of a malevolent spirit into the familiar domestic setting (which Arthur, particularly would recognise as being a safe haven via his own familial ties) bleeding the horror into the domestic. Likewise, the use of a new technology as a conduit for deceased voices raises the spectre of technologies as 'uncanny' and wider fears of technology as disrupter of the natural order (or 'techno fear').

Furthermore, the familiar in Kneale's work often turns out not to be familiar at all – be it the mutating form of the astronaut in *Quatermass*, the alien ancestors in *Quatermass and the Pit*, the ancient evil that negates any technology in *The Stone Tape*, or the sounds and landscapes of *TWIB*, nothing is necessarily as it seems. It is also clear that the spectral form of Janet is as sentient as anything in the supernatural realm, and her banshee-like shrieking an integral part of the corporeal fear she induces.

Kneale and techno-horror

Nigel Kneale himself was no stranger to time and technology as conduits of terror. Most famous as the creator of *Quatermass*, the interaction of technology and the unknown was explored in copious detail. The spaceman in the original series carries the literal and mental burden of his pioneering space travel, and is haunted by the changes wrought on his body and the slow degeneration into an organic state that results from this. From his encounters with technology, he literally loses the ability to be or resemble a human.

Likewise, the second series combines scientific experimentation with the loss of identity, with the mark of alien infiltration at the highest levels of British government.

The third series, *Quatermass and the Pit*, most famously reversed the paradigm of alien invasion by suggesting that humans were actually descendants of an earlier human race, while *The Quatermass Conclusion* likewise posited that megalithic stone circles were markers of evil for alien species harvesting human beings as energy (see Fryers and Harmes, forthcoming).

Much has been made of Kneale's rancorous involvement with *Halloween III: Season of the Witch* (1982), with Kneale himself at pains to distinguish the material he contributed from that which was subsequently added (most notably, the use of Stonehenge). The notion of broadcast television as a conduit for mass mayhem and murder was certainly in his original iterations, however, via a (heavily satirical) advert for Halloween toys that function as a ritual, sacrificial incantation.

It was Kneale's *The Stone Tape* (1972) which most obviously anticipated his treatment of technology in *TWIB*, as the one-off supernatural drama described a scenario in which stone monuments could function as recording devices for past events, replaying them at times of emotional trauma. A similar connection between technology and trauma is evident in many of the aforementioned texts in which aurality is a preoccupation – *The Road* being perhaps the most notable and dramatic.

In *TWIB*, sound also appears and recedes like the tide. The echoes of history are monstrous and menacing, but they serve as a reminder of inhumanity – of the forgotten, the oppressed, and the repressed. In *TWIB*, the recording discs open out the possibilities for technology as a repository of memories and a cathartic channel for dealing with the trauma of a haunting, with the widowed Mrs Drablow using them for both. The notion that the natural landscape can function as a recording for a traumatic event is also present in the 'calamity' that Arthur repeatedly hears on the causeway (although Mrs Drablow's recordings indicate that this is a contrivance of Janet to make her, and anyone else, suffer her pain). They also offer something new in this adaptation in giving a stoic, patrician, and aristocratic voice to a character without representation in the novella or any previous adaptation.

The recordings are a significant part of the retributive soundscape. Mrs Drablow's disembodied voice raises a notable series of connections and concerns in relation to empire and bodily subjectivity that likewise invites comparisons to gothic literature –

most notably Bram Stoker's *Dracula*. According to Judith Halberstam, 'The activities of reading and writing, then, are crucial in Dracula to the establishment of a kind of middle-class British hegemony and they are annexed to the production of sexual subjectivities' (1993: 336). Halberstam also quotes Wicke:

> The technology of the vampire's monstrosity, indeed, is intimately connected to the mode of the novel's production. As Jennifer Wicke has argued, Dracula is a veritable writing machine constructed out of diaries, letters, newspaper clippings, and medical case notes: 'Dracula, draped in all its feudalism and medieval gore, is textually completely au courant. Nineteenth-century diaristic and epistolary effusion is invaded by cutting-edge technology…'. (470, in Halberstam, 1993: 335)

Technology is a conduit through which identity is delineated. *TWIB* has a similar focus on written and recorded memory. For Straight, *Dracula* is concerned 'with how knowledge transfer and technology intersect with women's bodies and labor' (2017: 381). Part of Arthur's unravelling in the film is his interference in these records – his male presence in connection with these products of female memory transfer disturbs a dark history. The more he reads and the more he hears, the closer is his proximity to horror. In this, he is also a cypher for the reader of Stoker's and Hill's books and the audience of the film. Arthur's own voice on the discs, seemingly dismissive of this accumulated female history ('all Mrs Drablow's rubbish') and full of levity (cathartic whistling), echoes the protagonists of M. R. James's stories who, through a mixture of curiosity, disregard, and hubris, appear to enact their own catastrophe.

Straight also opines that Mina's writing and stenographic activities in *Dracula* become a way of protecting the British Empire from the invasive force of the titular Count, or 'the colonial other' (2017: 382). This will be explored in more detail in Chapter Five.

Here it is worth considering the similarities that the film shares with global screen cultures, in a circular relationship with each other. In the links between technology and terror, the wax discs serving as a conduit for past trauma, and electricity's association with the colonial classes (see Chapter Five), there are echoes of the text in the Japanese horror film *Ringu* (as well as Koji Suzuki's original novels and all their filmic and televisual iterations also suggested by Kim Newman, DVD commentary 2020). Although the vengeful wraith Sadako is intersex in the novel and is an incarnation of a sea deity, the original film and its Hollywood remake position the character as female, so as with the tradition of Onroyu in Japanese culture, it is thus emblematic of the repressed rage created by a deeply patriarchal culture.

Suzuki was influenced by the American horror *Poltergeist* (1982) in which the TV is a monstrous portal, and the scenes of the vengeful Sadako climbing out of the television gained iconic status (Anime News Network, no date). Likewise, *Ringu* director Hideo Nakata was inspired by Henry James's *The Turn of the Screw* and its British film adaptation, *The Innocents* (1961), as well as the British film *The Haunting* (1963) and the Hollywood blockbusters *The Exorcist* (1972) and the *Amityville Horror* films, stating 'I'd say the influence comes from Japanese as well as foreign directors' (Totaro, 2000). In an act of semiotic circularity, the 2012 film version of *TWIB* authored by Jane Goldman and directed by James Watkins was clearly influenced by the wave of J-horror (and more broadly, resurgent Asian horror) that proliferated in the new millennium, with the woman appearing and gliding in the manner of Asian wraiths (it is noteworthy, that in Kneale's own script, the woman moves 'sideways'), while Goldman's screenplay addition of the failed attempt by Arthur to lay the curse to rest by retrieving the boy's skeleton from the causeway mud mirrors the same failed attempt to assuage Sadako's rage by retrieving her bones from the well in *Ringu*.

In another interesting connection, Kneale conceived his original script for *Halloween III* as being about the electronic conveyance of ancient witchy curses:

> The theme was to be microchip witchcraft. In the old days, in order for a witch to put a curse on you, she had to make personal contact. With the advent of the microchip, a spell could be transferred through the Halloween gifts. A trademark stamp would carry the device and spread whatever evil influences it was designed to spread via a trigger mechanism incorporated into a TV programme. (Kneale, in Holliss, 1983: 31)

A female curse spread through technology precedes Suzuki's novel, Nakata's 'original' film, and later entries into the *Ring* franchise whereby the internet is used as a portal for Sadako's curse (from *Sadako*, 2012, onwards).

In Kneale's *TWIB* and *Ringu*, there is also a hope, later proven dramatically false, that the protagonists are safe and the curse averted. Both Janet's and Sadako's feminine rage cannot be assuaged by any means, only the moment of its impact delayed – the curse remains (in Suzuki's *Ringu*, it is a contagious virus triggered by a broadcast/video).

Another important similarity between the two texts is the link between time and space. *TWIB* is very much informed by time and tide taking on a monstrous form. In *Ringu*, the individuals cursed by viewing the videotape have a countdown of seven days before they are killed by Sadako (time is marked as claustrophobic, deathly, and inevitable), as displayed by a countdown that appears on screen. This is at the beckoning of what is essentially a sea demon. Again, by jettisoning the possibility of Arthur's survival, Kneale creates something similar here, and both deaths take on an aquatic form (via the tide and the lake), the significance of which will be explored in the next chapter, while the notion of maternal rage, which incorporates the menstrual and the amniotic, will be discussed in the final chapter.

In the end, and to Arthur's dismay, it turns out that indeed, both time *and* tide are waiting for at least one man.

Chapter Four: 'Just a house, on the marshes': Landscapes, Seascapes, and Horror

From soundscape to landscape: Arthur's utterance regarding Eel Marsh House ('Just a house...') may well be among the grossest understatements in British horror. The house and the landscape and seascape on which it sits are not just characters in their own right, but active, sentient, and menacing. Aside from the woman herself, they are the loci for death and tragedy. Arthur Kidd is equally compelled towards and repulsed away from them. As this chapter will elaborate, the spatial dynamics of Herbert Wise's film are essential ingredients in its evocation of horror, and simultaneously invite a range of questions regarding their specific use within a British context.

Chapter Three outlined the importance of temporality and sound in the film, factors linked to the landscapes and seascapes of the setting. The tide that engulfs the causeway and cuts it off from the land is regulated by the waxing and waning of the moon. Similar to Hill's original novel, landscapes, seascapes, and inland waterways all play an active part in Wise's adaptation. They fit the purpose of horror in being shifting and uneasily perceived; as will be explored, this adds to a sharp and unsettling distinction between what is seen and what isn't – and what is at one moment obscured and the next seen in alarming clarity. This chapter will explore the significance of space and place within *TWIB* – how these further relate both to notions of time and history and to other texts within a national and international framework.

McAndrew (2021) has offered a useful interdisciplinary understanding of the spaces of horror. Drawing on empirical studies from philosophy, psychology, and geography, he identifies our evolutionary instincts as being at the heart of our fear and unease in specific spaces that the horror genre habitually draws upon: old houses, graveyards, woodlands, bodies of water, and any place abandoned or devoid of human presence. These activate primary instincts such as agent detection mechanisms (2021) that are designed to protect us from predators and other evolutionary dangers. It is many of these spaces that this chapter will discuss which inform the 'horror' of *TWIB*.

The links between the landscape of East Anglia (the eastern English counties of Norfolk, Suffolk, Cambridgeshire, and Essex) where the film was partially filmed and British horror culture are now well-recognised (Armitt, 2018; Bacon and Whybray, 2021). More broadly, Hutchings (2004) and others have essayed the uses of the British landscape in horror and dark fantasy. These landscapes are rich in the connotations that McAndrew identifies.

Prior to this work, the emphasis was on the strain of British horror films that dealt with hidden instances of witchcraft, the occult, and broadly pagan practices such as the M. R. James adaptation *The Night of the Demon* (1957) or *The Wicker Man* (1973). In scholarship, the landscape emerged as a significant constituent in the 'Britishness' of texts and, furthermore, in their possibilities for subversion. Hunt labels these and other texts 'rural horror' (2002: 93): 'This green and pleasant land forever resists the onset of an age of reason' (2002: 86). For Krzywinska they also relate to a repressed history, with 'the landscape serving as a metaphor for the stratified layers of the collective unconscious' (2007: 81). Hutchings likewise labels these 'uncanny landscapes' which harbour troubling mysteries and horrors that uproot the very certainties of history and science. Due to the fact that rural drama has traditionally been associated with the more refined literary and costume dramas and the contested term 'heritage' texts, rural horrors stand in binary opposition as 'dark heritage' (Hutchings, 2004: 28).

The contemporary fascination with horror and the British landscape emanates to some degree from the BBC's celebrated adaptations of M. R. James's ghost stories. In the previous examples, and indeed in James, the use of the countryside is strongly established. As noted above, Susan Hill pays particular homage to James in her book and Kneale was also influenced by him, and it is almost inevitable that this accumulation of influences and antecedents would bleed through into Wise's adaptation.

Some examples from the BBC's adaptations clarify these points. For Easterbrook, 'a sense of isolation is integral to Clark's adaptation' of 'A Warning to the Curious' (2012: 11), while for Mark Fisher

> The BBC adaptations [of M. R. James] are remarkable for their attention to place. The camera lingers on the eerily empty Norfolk and Suffolk landscapes, which become in many ways the most significant agency in the television films. (2012: 21)

The actual, tidal location of Eel Marsh House is Osea Island and causeway on the Thames Estuary in Essex, placing it both within the larger environs of East Anglia and within the insidious tidal reach of the North Sea, spiritually, as well as literally linking it with the haunted landscapes of M. R. James. (The house itself is sited elsewhere, however, and was inserted into this landscape via a glass shot.)

The ghost stories of James were strongly informed by specific locales along the East Anglian coast which in turn were replicated in the attention to landscape in the 1970s adaptations filmed along the same stretch of coastline. Susan Hill was influenced by both James and the same coastline. Inspiration for the novella came from an extended stay in a Suffolk house that adjoined the sea. Hill's later horror novella *Dolly* (2012) also features Iyot Lock – a creaky old house in the fens of East Anglia.

The same stretch of desolate coastline has attracted other horror filmmakers. The horror film *Afterdeath* (2015) visited the coastal village of Happisburgh where *A Warning to the Curious* was filmed, and the science-fiction/horror hybrid *Annihilation* (2018) was filmed among the same patch of sandy pine trees at Holkham as *AWTC*. Jonathan Miller's adaptation of M. R. James – *Whistle and I'll Come to You* (1968) – was filmed at Waxham beach on the north Norfolk coast. Other notable horror films made in the East Anglia region include *The Witchfinder General* (1968), *The Reeds* (2010), *Possum* (2018), and *Widow's Walk* (2019). These examples position the coast and waterways of the region as repositories for ghosts and death.

A rarer example exists in the cerebral drama *Do Not Disturb* (1991), a title that could equally apply to any number of M. R. James's stories. This play by Timberlake Wertenbaker was for the *Screen Two* strand of one-off dramas. The shifting and restless coastal plains of north Norfolk become a metaphor for the protagonist's attempt to unravel the life and death of an elusive writer of ghost stories.

Local legend and folklore abound in this area, from the ghost of a murdered smuggler thrown down a well in Happisburgh and the slavering hound of hell Black Shuck to the ghostly church bells of the lost town of Dunwich. Hill's novella talks of 'drowned churches and the swallowed up village' (1983: 35). The Anglia TV production *The Uninvited* (1997) posited that the sunken village was the site of insidious alien activity.

The great flood of 1953 which claimed the lives of 326 people underscores that the region is also a site of corporeal death.

At Cromer, it was the tale of Black Shuck and the imposing façade of Cromer Hall that were said to have provided inspiration for Conan Doyle's *The Hound of the Baskervilles*. On the same coast, an avenging spirit from beyond the grave draws two illicit lovers to the clifftop in E. F. Benson's 'The Dance'. For MacFarlane, this is a landscape which 'snags, bites and troubles' (in Armitt, 2018: 291).

Further up the East coast and still adjacent to the North Sea is Scarborough, the Yorkshire seaside resort where Susan Hill grew up and where the stage play of *TWIB* premiered. In recent years, its faded charms have provided the backdrop to the TV horror miniseries *Remember Me* (2014) and the sinister *Saint Maude* (2019). Further north still, the port of Whitby was the location at which Count Dracula disembarked from his murderous sojourn aboard the *Demeter*. It also served as the backdrop to the 1977 BBC adaptation of Stoker's novel.

However, it is further south that immediately concerns us – Essex. Osea Island and its causeway to be precise. Cult horror director Ben Wheatley was raised in Essex and was inspired in his career choice by the natural landscape: 'There was something in the land-scape that plainly terrified me… If you went out into it you could just be killed' (quoted in Armitt, 2018: 291, originally in MacFarlane, 2015). Osea island is accessible only via the causeway, and as such, has been another space habitually haunted by British horror films, appearing also in *Unhappy Birthday* (2011), *Writer's Retreat* (2015), and *Dogged* (2017) – texts in which the isolated island space is an excuse to entrap the protagonists.

As with the bucolic landscape and the perpetual coastline, islands invite suggestions of the eldritch – the weird, sinister, or ghostly – by nature of their isolation, as well as offering a dark or alternative history of the British Isles. The state of being an island means that the sea informs everything Britain does as a nation – it can be a moat around the kingdom or a conduit through which to attack it. While popular texts have traditionally ignored the latter in favour of celebrating the former, horror and fantasy texts articulate the fears inherent in potential vulnerability.

While by no means the exclusive preserve of British culture, the damned, haunted, and demonic island has particular relevance for Great Britain as a country so readily projected as an island nation with an isolationist outlook. The island offers an apposite metaphor for Britain. The island also holds symbolic resonance within British arts and culture, with its provenance in British literature from Shakespeare's *The Tempest* through horror, fantasy, and science fiction (and their hybridised elements), as in H. G. Wells' *The Island of Doctor Moreau* (1896). Similarly, the island has strong connections with mythology and folklore, most obviously evidenced through the Isle of Avalon from Arthurian legend.

Fictional new island communities that diverge from the 'island paradise' or adventure paradigm are usually depicted as sick perversions of the 'known' precepts of law and religion, or extreme and unchecked examples of such (as in William Golding's *Lord of the Flies* and Robin Hardy's *The Wicker Man*). The island at the end of the Nine Lives Causeway is both connected and unconnected to the mother country. It follows that country's laws and logic but also follows its own.

The capacity of the island to function either as a safe haven from the contamination (literal and figurative) of the mainland, buffeted by the sea, or as a quarantine area in the opposite direction is explored in *Doomwatch* (1972) and *Night of the Big Heat* (1967), as well as in recent examples of zombie contamination such as *The Rezort* (2015). The effect of isolation, quarantine, and fear of infection is focused on a small group of individuals but writ large as an example of what may occur to the larger population of the island state. As will be explored, this has connotations for *TWIB* in questions of malignant and tainted private histories becoming publicly exposed and spread.

In other examples, the island is literally a 'foreign' place and a dangerous 'other' space in the hinterland between the mother country and another culture (and the spiritual realm), as with the fog-shrouded Jersey of *The Others* (2001). The fact that the sea produces an island only intermittently in *TWIB* also suggests a destabilisation of certainty that is exacerbated by the shifting fog and the unreliable sonic landscape. All of these factors, individual or combined, produce a powerful alienation in Arthur and the audience – an accumulation of the spaces which create horrific ambiguity.

The text thus offers a triple jeopardy: Eel Marsh House represents the haunted house in English culture, it is embedded in a haunted landscape (with a graveyard for added measure), and it also exists as an island space, cut off from the mainland (but only sometimes). Part of this environment is the fog or 'frets', which bring further instability and a further inhibition to being able to see with clarity – they bring further ambiguity. According to Bacon and Whybray, 'Instead of fog, East Anglia has sea frets that blur instead of blanket, rendering the edges of things incomplete or invisible' (2021: 219). The obtuse behaviour of frets is laid out plainly by the local businessman Sam Toovey:

> Them dense patches of sea fog, now those can distort sound, blanket some off and let others through… You're a townie – you don't know what a gull can sound like. They can make cries you'd swear came from, say, a cat, or a baby.

This inability to see and the duplicitousness of the natural environment are evident in the novella: Arthur was a man who 'clung to the prosaic, the invisible and the tangible' (Hill, 1983: 12) but Eel Marsh and its environs disrupt this: 'they seemed to stretch in every direction, as far as I could see, and to merge without a break into the waters of the estuary' (1983: 53). There are further connections with the text and with the 1970s M. R. James adaptations, *Lost Hearts* (1973) in particular. Ramsey Campbell opines that 'There is a difference between real fog and the studio variety, and *Lost Hearts* demonstrates it. Here, it's palpable enough to chill the bones, it's an essence of the landscape, and, it seems, the vengeful dead who appear to bring it with them' (2012: 16). Again, this could equally be applied to the manner in which the frets bring terror in *TWIB*. What is also clear is that the environment takes on what Easterbrook, describing *A Warning to the Curious*, defines as a form of 'dark impressionism' (2012: 13).

Tidal energy is also a crucial part of the landscape of terror in the text, and one that has been associated with death from at least the time of Aristotle. Armitt (2018: 298) reminds us that the ebb tide is associated with death within British culture, quoting marine scientist David Pugh: 'Even as recently as 1595, Parish Registers in the Hartlepool area… recorded the phase of the tide along with the date and time of each death' (Pugh, 2004: 27 in Armitt, 2018: 298). The deaths on the tidal causeway would suggest that the death actually took place at high tide rather than at low or ebb tide, but the reminders of the event that haunt Arthur tend to do so at ebb tide, such as during the day or when Keckwick comes to collect him. Either way, *TWIB* forms part of a long tradition of North Sea death and British culture, and everything about Eel Marsh House and its environs emphasises this. The perpetual ebb and flow associated with such spaces also serve as a potent metaphor for the ebbing fortunes of humanity, while the titular woman cuts across this with her unbounded ferocity.

The graveyard itself is an obvious example of a place of decay that has taken on the function of death within social discourse. The graveyard also has a contemplative association, derived from texts such as Thomas Gray's *Elegy Written in a Country Churchyard* (1750). It is a place discussed in hushed, reverent, or proto-conspiratorial tones. *TWIB* signals this as it features not one but two graveyards, and these are the space from which the woman and the haunting manifests. The graveyard by the sea is a step further. It suggests restless death, part of maritime spaces within the horror genre which 'provide confusion as to recognised limits or boundaries' (Fryers, 2021a). If the seaside is a place of shifting space and temporality, then the coastal grave suggests that this restlessness continues after physical death – it is a place of 'double' or 'hyper liminality' (Fryers, 2021a) and a place in which McAndrew's 'ambiguity' dominates. Slippages between stable and unstable landscapes and material and immaterial presence create the pockets of uncertainty where horror thrives in the text.

Churches revisited

It is once again the process of looking that proves Arthur's misfortune – looking at the graves signals the woman's appearance – as if the act of his looking is a violation of their sanctity and an explanation for her enmity.

As per the novella, there are two church buildings on the screen in *TWIB*, one intact (the parish church where Kidd attends Mrs Drablow's funeral) and the other ruined (the remains of the abbey out on the marshes, near Eel Marsh House). Kneale faithfully follows Hill in using both, although in his own writing he was already sensitive to the way the ecclesiastical and the uncanny could potently combine, a manner showing M. R. James's influence on Kneale's imagination. Westminster Abbey is the scene of the climax in *The Quatermass Experiment* and a church in London is one of the signifiers (through its 'hobgoblin' grotesques) of Martian race memory in *Quatermass and the Pit*. Key scenes in *TWIB* take place in and around churches.

The ruined abbey is a gaunt sight. The east wall of the vanished church still stands, with its single large and empty window, the jagged remains of tracery looking like the stumps of broken teeth. The grey stone blends with the mist. Monastic remains could be picturesque and indeed inspired romantic-era paintings of moonlit ruins. The composition of Wise's shot of Kidd and the woman against the ruin in fact evokes Carl Gustav Carus's *Ruine bei Mondschein*. But English monastic ruins, where windows denuded of glass and tracery look like gaping mouths, give the imaginative anthropomorphic impression they are screaming faces.

The parish church is well maintained and looks homely and comforting, as is often the case with English country churches. But the ghostly violates the sacredness of both ecclesiastical sites. The gaping maw on the marshes and the parish church are important sites where the woman in black appears to menace Kidd. In the church's graveyard Kidd notes something unsettling: an unnaturally large number of graves of children. Out in the abbey, he sees a visual link between the two sites at another grave, the woman's own gravestone. In a visual cause and effect, the grave at the abbey marks where the woman is buried but not resting, and her active malevolence is the cause of the many deceased children in the other graveyard.

In book and television film, the ecclesiastical settings are continuations of a recent but evocative television tradition. Traditionally stringent guidelines (especially at the BBC) prohibited television programs using churches for anything other than wholesome purposes, a point famously made clear by the 1971 *Doctor Who* serial *The Dæmons*, which could only show scenes of a devil-worshipping vicar and satanic cult in the crypt of a church, not in the church building proper. However, by the mid-1970s these were relaxing and the BBC's *A Ghost Story for Christmas* made memorable use of ecclesiastical settings. Norwich Cathedral became Barchester Cathedral in the 1971 adaptation of M. R. James's 'The Stalls of Barchester Cathedral' (broadcast as *The Stalls of Barchester*). The adaptation in 1974 of 'The Treasure of Abbot Thomas' made extensive use of Wells Cathedral in Somerset and St Mary's Church in Orchardleigh. St Mary's Church in Happisburgh stood in as the parish church in Seaburgh in *A Warning to the Curious* in 1972, with the actual mediaeval porch serving as part of the production design as characters discuss its symbolism (the same church appears in *Do Not Disturb*).

These filming locations follow the descriptive cues of James's stories, in which churches and their fabric are direct participants in the supernatural. The choir stalls of Barchester Cathedral are not static items carved from dead wood, but dynamically and preternaturally living objects, carrying foreboding warnings. Ancient stained glass in 'Abbot Thomas' is a key to a mediaeval mystery. Although he was not a clergyman himself, James was a child of the rectory and his career as school master, don, and bibliographer enmeshed him in ecclesiastical environments surrounded by ancient gothic fabrics. In many stories, not merely those filmed by the BBC, the fabric of old churches is intrinsic to preternatural menace. The churches themselves are frequently sites of the unholy. In 'An Uncommon Prayerbook', perverted rubrics in the *Book of Common Prayer* are the cause of ghostly menace, and suggestions of the unholy cling to Southminster Cathedral in 'An Episode of Cathedral History' and the cathedral close at Whitminster in 'The Residence at Whitminster'. These cues inform the two ecclesiastical settings in *TWIB*, both as holy places in the landscape violated by the unholy.

Spaces

A consideration of the use of spaces in *TWIB* inevitably draws comparisons to the novel, radio, stage, and cinematic iterations of the text, which again points to discussions of cinematic and televisual aesthetics. Sarah Cardwell (2015) cautions against the prevalent dichotomy within film and television studies (and, indeed, beyond) that views rectangular widescreen (16:9 ratios) as inherently cinematic and the traditional squarer television ratio (4:3) as less expansive. This is bound up with questions and debates surrounding the 'quality' of television in comparison to film – a much-debated concept within screen studies. As this book has elaborated, there are no barriers to either viewers or scholars regarding a televisual text as 'cinematic', nor is there necessarily a distinction in quality between the two, merely differences in how they are *perceived*. As previously argued, *TWIB* represents the 'best of both (or multiple) worlds' in many regards and the following analysis will demonstrate how the specific use of spaces within *TWIB* is crucial to the production of meaning and effect.

Figures 4 and 5 are a useful illustration of Cardwell's argument that televisual aesthetics offer an alternative rather than an impoverished use of spatial dynamics. The same scene – Arthur Kidd's first journey with Keckwick in the pony and trap to Eel Marsh House – is represented in the original broadcast format of 4:3 (Figure 4, with black bars demarcating the edge of the frame) and in a 16mm print in the 'cinematic' aspect ratio of 16:9 (Figure 5) that Network's 2020 DVD release included. The first thing to notice is the vertical nature of the framing, which shows a cross-country view of the countryside, paying attention to the horizontal layers, colours, and textures, with the characters almost invisible and insignificant within the landscape. While the 16:9 ratio offers more space on the edges of the frame, given the vertical composition, there is more space on the y-axis at the top and bottom of the frame in the original aspect ratio, arguably enhancing the isolation of the trap against the sky.

This would tally with Cardwell's thesis (2015) that televisual aesthetics are equally important and that a wider landscape framing does not necessarily offer anything better or more expressive (arguably the latter, in this regard). Panos and Lacey suggest a similar view and advocate for the 'complexity of televisual language' (2015: 2).

Figures 4 and 5. Framing in 4:3 (Figure 4) and 16:9 (Figure 5) – both indicate verticality in the composition. In both, the landscape is equally significant.

The visual language of *TWIB* is complex. The choices of framing and composition throughout the text are deliberate and create a sense of character, regulate mood and tone, and contribute to a sense of entrapment and impending doom. They have a particular rhythm of their own and fluctuate in the same manner as the causeway. On top of this, as indicated, the locations function of their own volition.

Many texts juxtapose metropolitan and rural spaces to emphasise the open nature of the former with the claustrophobic nature of the latter in a centrifugal manner (e.g., film noir – see Dimendberg, 2004). Horror texts often do the opposite and are centripetal – the further away from the city the characters get, the less the rules of civilisation (and by extension, safety) operate. *TWIB* tends towards the former, but also balances them for dramatic effect.

Early scenes of London are represented as not overcrowded but busy enough to suggest the lively working life of the capital (the relative emptiness may be from budgetary considerations as well). Wise tightly frames scenes in Arthur's house – one particular shot from the top of the staircase looking down is unsettling in that it suggests claustrophobia and the act of being watched from afar. But the film balances these with scenes of cheery domesticity, hinting that domestic spaces can equally represent freedom and restriction depending on the viewpoint.

Wise also tightly frames the scenes of the railway station and carriages of Arthur's journey to Crythin Gifford – an early indicator that the seaside may not be a place of escape. Scenes of the tavern and Gifford market day are also tightly framed and contain far more people than the London scenes, reversing the dichotomy of sleepy village and urban chaos.

The inn is especially tightly framed and full of detail (as is Pepperell's office). In this regard, it echoes the inns and taverns of Hammer Horror films, noted for their 'busy' mise-en-scene. In line with the traditional horror or thriller film, low camera angles are employed – Wise films scenes of the house, railway station, pony and trap, and others from this perspective to create an uncanny or menacing feel.

The early scene of the funeral is an excellent example of the rhythmic and expressive use of framing, composition, and camera movement in *TWIB*, aesthetics that help set the text apart from more pedestrian adaptations, and which compare favourably with the 2012 Hammer adaptation. Wise shoots external scenes acutely to create tension while the interior of the church is framed in long shots – to emphasise the loneliness of the event and to give space for spirits to emerge.

The geometric composition of the external shots displaces secure notions of daytime space and hints that the spirit of the woman is expected less at night than in the daytime. This creates the effect that all daytime scenes have pregnant menace alongside the nocturnal scenes more commonly associated with manifestations. Wise often frames these scenes on a diagonal axis to emphasise this, to create a sense of unease even in wide shots. This switches between other framings, notably through the church's lychgate, which adds to the tension.

The camera movement is equally fluid and revealing. A subtle tracking shot initially reveals the ghost among the gravestones. The ghost disappears and then reveals herself again before disappearing once more as Arthur and Mr Pepperell traverse the frame from left to right. Wise again deploys this subtle use of blocking and camera movement to adumbrate the manifestation and de-manifestation of a spirit when Arthur again encounters the woman amongst the graves in the grounds of Eel Marsh House. Her appearance tied to his movement links her presence, and his subsequent fate, inexplicably to Arthur and his place within the environment. Thus, space and environment are central preoccupations in this iteration.

Fittingly, for a visual medium, much of the text's energy comes from the act of looking. Arthur cannot prevent himself from looking when he first sees the woman in the church – he hasn't become accustomed to averting his gaze as the vicar and Pepperell do. After this, he is condemned to see, and the viewer is also condemned to see what he sees by association. Another useful link here is with M. R. James's 'The Mezzotint', of which Armitt describes the combination of 'seeing and not seeing' (2018: 296) as being central to manifesting terror. Similarly, the assertion that 'it is the landscape that proves crucial in connecting the living and the dead' in Kate Mosse's 'The Revenant' (2014) applies with equal conviction here (Armitt, 2018: 297).

It is while looking at the graves of the woman's dead relatives that Janet's presence is conjured again, as though the act of casually glancing at the past is an intrusion on the act of grief. Arthur's 'looking' is emphasised by a low angle as he glances over the gravestone and again as he surveys the landscape (we don't see what he does here yet, creating tension). His compulsion to look is emphasised as he walks back towards the house but suddenly stops, and spins around. It is here that the powerful and destructive female gaze (see Chapter Six) is emphasised as the epicentre of the film's horror.

The first close-up of her face conveys menace. Gradually, the woman gets closer and closer, closing the literal and metaphorical gap between them, and their destinies are further entwined. It is also her gaze that holds the power of life and death. This is evident through composition and editing, best exemplified by the switches between wide shots and medium close-ups of Arthur and the woman to close-ups of their facial expressions. She gets closer to him through camerawork and editing. In the second medium close-up, she steps towards the edges of the frame and also gets closer to the audience. (Compare this with Sadako's televisual eruption in *Ringu*.) Arthur physically retreats at this point, but this only serves to delay the moment of contact which Wise renders in shocking form during 'that' later scene of the woman bearing down on him on the bed. He places his hands over his eyes – once again only forestalling the curse which eventually follows him to London. (There are links to *Ringu* again here, which is also predicated on an act of 'watching', in this case the cursed video.)

The link between the act of 'looking' and the invocation of terror has its basis in our everyday activities. Studies have indicated that eye contact influences our levels of trust and connection to each other, with 'unusual patterns of eye contact' or 'unusual facial features, especially in the region of the eyes' listed among characteristics that put us on high alert – an 'ambiguity of threat' (McAndrew, 2021). The gaunt, pale appearance of the woman which draws attention to her intense and hateful eyes carries these precepts to heightened levels.

The occasional and deliberate use of tracking shots gives the text a cinematic feel (if that is the right word, considering Cardwell's cautions on that front) and helps open out the spaces of the narrative at opportune moments where it was consciously restricted before. In a text about seeing that the framing often makes difficult, we are occasionally asked to see with great clarity. Potent examples of this are scenes within Eel Marsh House. First is a scene in which Arthur, traumatised by repeated exposure to the calamity on the causeway, struggles to close the front door. The camera tracks backwards along the corridor, revealing the empty house as animated through the wind (light fittings swinging) while Arthur gets gradually smaller within the frame – emphasising his isolation and trauma.

The second significant scene occurs in Arthur's last moments within the house, as he and Sam enter the nursery. The camera tracks around the spaces of the nursery at a violent pace, revealing the destruction of the room, and heightening the impact of that revelation.

Pagan and rural horrors often make deliberate use of a landscape's expansiveness as a means of distinguishing it from the claustrophobia of the urban environment and as an alternative type of restriction and oppression. *TWIB* doesn't fully follow this dichotomy, partially, as we have seen, as an effect of its televisual aesthetics. The frets obscure even the expansive shots of the causeway, which exacerbates the feeling that Kidd is being drawn into a spider's web, creating ambiguities of space and place.

Dark and lonely waters

Within horror, the use of space is often about more than purely aesthetic concerns, but provokes wider questions of fear and national cultures. Alongside the coast and countryside, inland waters are places of death in *TWIB*. The river trip has attained a special status within British culture – for freedom, gaiety, and whimsy. 'Messing about on the river' is an embedded part of British cultural life, embodied in Kenneth Grahame's *The Wind in the Willows* and Jerome K. Jerome's *Three Men in a Boat*, for example (Fryers, 2021a). Lewis Carroll conceived of *Alice in Wonderland* on a gentle Sunday river trip in the Oxfordshire countryside. In British film, the waterside picnic – a romantic escape from the restrictions of the city or the gossip of the small town – is a trope present in a range of films from *Brief Encounter* (1945) to *Alfie* (1966).

But as with Hutching's uncanny landscapes, the peaceful river has its antitheses. British crime film and television are awash with corpses dredged up from rivers and inland waters – the Thames being a habitual and especial offender (*The Dark Eyes of London* or *Frenzy*, for example). Ponds, rivers, lakes, sluices, canals, quarries, and all manner of moving or static aquatic repositories are places of death.

Yet the tendency goes back further still. Inland drownings haunt British literature – Ophelia in *Hamlet*, Maggie and Tom Tulliver in *The Mill on the Floss*, or Rosanna Spearman in *The Moonstone* are famous examples. Dorothy L. Sayers' 1934 detective novel *The Nine Tailors* is set in fenland bloated by floods. The 1974 BBC adaptation was filmed at the massive Norfolk church Walpole St Peter, with Foul Anchor Sluice used as the site of a drowning. Outside of fiction, British rivers claimed the lives of the Tudor composer Robert Parsons, who drowned in the flooded River Trent in 1572, and of Virginia Woolf, who walked into the River Ouse with stones in her pockets. Smaller bodies of water could be lethal. The Victorian lyricist W. S. Gilbert drowned in the lake of his country home, Grim's Dyke, trying to rescue a girl from drowning. The village pond and other aquatic spaces were also places where women were dunked as punishment or if they were accused of being a witch, actions memorably depicted in *The Avengers: Murdersville* (1967) and *The Witchfinder General* (1968). These spaces are equally associated with diablerie as they are with levity.

There is tragedy, but a patina of romance attached to the tradition, as best exemplified by Pre-Raphaelite painter Sir John Everett Millais's famous evocation of Ophelia's death (1851–52). More recent examples include Graham Swift's *Waterland* and Michel Paver's *Wakenhyrst*. Susan Hill's later ghost story *Dolly*, from 2012, is similarly set in a 'decaying house deep in the damp, lonely fens' (book jacket synopsis, 2012), to which the protagonist, much like the author, is compelled to return.

The 1970s were a particular period in which popular imagination imbricated British inland waters as a place of death. The short public information film *The Spirit of Dark and Lonely Water* (1973) most obviously expressed this point. Dead, orphaned children with missing organs haunt the rivers and dykes of *Lost Hearts* (1973), a family tragedy on the river blights *The Asphyx* (1972) and *Voices* (1973), while a similar catastrophe haunts the parents all the way to the waterways of Venice in *Don't Look Now* (1973). All these were released within a year of each other, and one could speculate that this fear of losing children may be a legacy of the previous decade's counterculture and generational tensions. Statistics on drowning that stimulated the production of *Lonely Water* (Fryers, 2020) offer a more mundane answer. As McAndrew explains,

> Physical features that posed a threat to our ancestors can easily become creepy, even if they have other qualities that make them beneficial to us; water is a perfect example of an indispensable and usually attractive element of a natural setting that is frequently associated with horror. Rivers, lakes, and ponds often provide the setting for horror stories about ghosts. This makes sense in that deep water has always posed a hazard to humans and drowning is a common cause of human death, both accidental and intentional. (2021)

TWIB, therefore, offers another strand to its nostalgic impulses in evoking a long and recent propensity for water and violent death. It is significant that one of Kneale's most important interventions in *TWIB* would be to turn boating on the river into a place of death. In Hill's novella, Arthur is drawn into the marsh to rescue Spider and both almost drown as the woman looks on from Eel Marsh House. As outlined in Chapter Two, Kneale's is a definitive ending that sweeps away ambiguity. As also noted, the appearance of the woman, hovering on the surface of the water, also offers a dark, biblical inversion of Christ walking on the water – something that likely heightens its dramatic impact.

These scenes also echo visually the 1961 adaptation of Henry James's *The Turn of the Screw*, *The Innocents*, in which the previous governess drowned herself in the lake and manifests as a ghost, dressed in black and standing on the surface of the water among the reeds (or, ambiguously, as a figment of the new governess's fevered psyche). In the original novella, the visitation appears by the pond, not actually on it. Audio-visual forbears influence visual as much as do the literary ones. In Kneale's first draft, the aquatic death is even more pronounced. In saving Kidd, in line with the novella, he has to witness the chilling death of his family. As we discussed in Chapter Two, in the script's first draft he finds them on the river bed:

> 137. Underwater
>
> He finds his family.
>
> STELLA, still clutching the baby but crushed and dead, with open eyes.
> And then EDDIE, floating deep and trapped… (105)

There is a circularity of reference points again here as *The Turn of the Screw* inspired Susan Hill in writing her novella, itself inspired by Charlotte Brontë's *Jane Eyre* (1847)

– and later, *The Innocents* inspired Hideo Nakata's *Ringu* (1998). Director of *The Innocents*, Jack Clayton, also consulted Nigel Kneale at an early stage of the script's development, given Kneale's reputation for handling fantastic and supernatural material (Murray, 2017: 117).

Trains and trauma

There are two other important facets of Arthur's literal journey that are worth examining as they relate to British landscape, culture, and history. When Arthur returns to London and his period of convalescence, his son asks him 'you've been to the seaside?' Arthur responds in surprise to this: 'Did I? I suppose I did, I never thought of it like that'. His inability to make the connection between his experiences in Crythin Gifford and this British cultural tradition is once again due largely to the disruptive effect created by the gothic/horror tradition. The tradition of seaside holidays first began in the nineteenth century with royal patronage of Scarborough, Brighton, and other locales, and later transformed into a great working-class tradition. We see inverted versions of the carefree seaside trip in both adaptations of M. R. James's 'Oh, Whistle…' (1968 and 2010) as well as non-horror texts such as *The Birthday Party* (1968) in which we encounter what Allen describes as the 'limits of liminality' (2008).

This disconnect is exacerbated by the fact that Crythin Gifford as an audio-visual space is also not evident as a seaside village. The sounds of the sea, the marshes, and the marine wildlife that are present at the house and causeway are absent from the village, which much more closely resembles the inland location that it actually is (Lacock in Wiltshire). The ability of film to fuse spaces together can also create schisms in the way that it does so, but this also serves the purpose of deliberate estrangement that is part of the mechanics of horror – whether as artful or happy coincidence.

The ability for masses of the country to travel to the seaside became possible by the introduction of the railways in the nineteenth century. These opened up freedom and possibilities, and likewise gained their own associations with romance that transferred suitably to British film (for example, *Night Mail*). Yet, once again, the genre opens up the possibility for a dark twin. Armitt (2018) identifies such a strain in the English ghost story, especially Charles Dickens' 'The Signalman'. Armitt quotes Catherine Aird in suggesting that as well as possibilities, the opening of the railways also brought with it fear and potential trauma, including what was termed 'commotion shock' (Aird, 2012: 25 in Armitt, 2018: 294), something that Dickens himself personally channelled, having survived the Staplehurst rail disaster in 1865.

This is likewise present in the adaptation of tales by James and Dickens, notably *A Warning to the Curious*, where they are spaces of manifestation. Therefore, denuded of its association with the freedom and gaiety of the seaside trip, the train journey is a channel which brings Arthur closer to horror and mortality – something that a return journey cannot assuage.

This brings us back to considerations and configurations of death and trauma and the landscape. The 'alluvial' nature (Bacon and Whybray, 2021) of the East Anglia region and the connections to earlier folk texts are re-emphasised by the tidal discourse of the causeway in *TWIB*. Armitt proposes that the ghost stories of M. R. James, embedded as they are in the landscape of the East Anglian region, give expression to existential threats of coastal (or 'ghost-al', in Armitt's idiom) erosion and, by extension in modern contexts, climate change: the stories 'provides us with a mechanism for giving shape to otherwise formless cultural anxieties' (2016: 97).

Armitt suggests that human intervention, not necessarily climatic change, is responsible for erosion on the East coast, from mediaeval drainage to the establishment of the coastal resort, which drove humans 'closer to the shoreline' (2016: 95–96), and that this is not a new phenomenon. It is human behaviour, not simply the elements, which has created a situation in which the sea devours the land. Likewise, the final manifestation of the shape in James's 'Oh, Whistle…' occurs as the merciless North Sea wind lashes the windows of the hotel: 'Whether natural or supernatural in form, James's fiend may originate from the shoreline, but it takes its real force from the storm surge' (2016: 102). It may be argued that similar human agency gave birth to the destructive enmity of the woman in black, as she bursts forth from the landscape into the human world and engineers the aural haunting that creeps menacingly in with the sea and its frets.

Armitt concludes that 'The very act of considering the relationship between ghosts and geography reminds us of how miniscule an individual human lifetime is in comparison with the landscape' (2018: 299). The ghost story thus haunts us with this unassailable fact, while the ghost connected with the sea and the tides similarly layers a fear of destructive nature and the destructive nature of humanity on top of this. Further, the destabilisation of time, space, and place provides an erasure of certainty, and calls into question foundational myths, something upon which the next chapter will elaborate.

Chapter Five: 'Mr Drablow was a China trader, he died out East': Colonialism and National Identity

It is clear from the last chapters that time and place are integral factors in establishing the depth and complexity of the production, central in creating meaning and, last but not least, in creating a pervasive sense of dread. The ebbs and flows of the causeway are a perfect metaphor for history – constant progress and regression. This chapter will continue where the previous one left off, exploring in more detail the significance of the time, place, and history the film evokes, opening out questions about where societal horror lies in connection with the horror evoked in the text, and in its specific British historical context.

The term 'China trader' is a throwaway statement, an almost unnecessary background detail to help add some context to the Drablow family – their presence, spectral through absence and the mention of death in a foreign land (the novella alludes to relatives in India). Yet it suggests so much about the Drablow family and their history – the money that built Eel Marsh House and the relations between the Drablows and the town of Crythin Gifford. Discussing anything relating to the British Empire is rarely straightforward and is primed with pregnant meaning and meta-detail. It is also indicative of another authorial addition by Nigel Kneale that adds scale and scope to this film.

Even after its dissolution, the British Empire has long retained an influence on British national life and top-down formations of British national identity. Kipling's 'The White Man's Burden' is viewed with far more circumspection in a contemporary context, yet the fact that the 'sun never set' on the British Empire means that its influence on internal and global affairs is still tangible even if vestigial.

There is always a dark double to dominant myths, and horror is exceptional in giving expression to this. The last chapter demonstrated that the myths of the 'green and pleasant land' and the 'sceptre'd isle' are uprooted through the scrupulous lens of horror, and triumphant imperial myths are no different. Even at the height of the Empire, horror and gothic texts were providing a form of counternarrative to uncomplicated notions of colonial national identity. Horror texts peered behind the curtain of the dominant myths and, unconsciously or otherwise, gave expression to the dark forces that dominant ideologies work so hard to suppress.

Stoker's *Dracula* revealed a heightened awareness of invasion or contamination of the mother country, while Richard Marsh's *The Beetle* (1897) and Stoker's own *The Jewel of the Seven Stars* (1903), both products of the late Victorian and Edwardian 'Egyptomania' and the 'Imperial Gothic', envisaged the discontents of the colonies wreaking their revenge, and general invasion and pollution by 'foreigners'. Tales of mystics, curses, and cursed objects from foreign lands informed W. W. Jacobs' *The Monkey's Paw* and would be a consistent motif in British horror film and television from the 1919 adaptation of *The Beetle*, through *The Ghoul* (1932) and *Hellraiser* (1987), to *Remember Me* (2014). As will be suggested with regards to *TWIB*, the capacity for horror to be generated within the self – or at least within a colonising nation state – is also present in all these texts.

Nineteenth-century trade with China was not an equal system of trading but facilitated by war and coercion. With increased demand for high-end goods such as silk, porcelain, and tea, and a lack of silver to trade for them with the Qing Dynasty, British merchants looked to use Indian opium instead. Between 1790 and 1832, China was flooded with cheap opium, causing widespread addiction and social degradation. (A relatable, if shocking, metaphor might be the relations between a pimp and their sex workers, where drugs are used to engender dependence and acquiescence.) In response to this, imported opium was banned and destroyed, prompting the First Opium War in 1839, which extended and legitimised aggressive trading in the country. Historian H. C. G. Matthew describes this as 'the most disreputable of all Britain's imperialistic exploits, as it was a considered and consistent policy, not the accidental result of a local crisis' (1993: 506).

In this context, the term 'China trader' is not just one of laudable individual enterprise, but brings with it a conundrum of implicit meanings related to violence, death, coercion, and exploitation. Eel Marsh House, the comfortable existence of the Drablows, and their private history are therefore a legacy of this suppressed public history. The absence in this iteration (or indeed any iteration) of any non-Caucasian characters or performers (or indeed crew behind the camera) underscores this visible absence (although ethnic otherness is implicit in the inclusion of gypsy characters discussed later). Mr Drablow, another largely off-screen presence, is also spectral – seen only in an old photograph. (Kneale's script describes him, appropriately, as 'pompous looking'.)

The house is a legacy of death and oppression in varying contexts and a repository for objects which speak to that. Like atrocities that take place outside the confines of the page in virtually any other nineteenth-century text, in narratives like *TWIB* they occur off screen, but their context and presence are felt in the lives and actions of the characters – even the dead ones.

In interpreting the non-fiction work of Dickens, in particular his visit to America, Smith recognises a form of colonial gothic. In slavery he reads the mutilated and branded bodies of the slaves as signs of a culture which has generated horror from within and created the potential for national self-destruction (2010: 148). Seen in this light, it is realistic to interpret the unrestrained rage of Janet as a cumulative force generated by the Drablows' own colonial exploits. It is a force that upturns society.

Eel Marsh House

According to Tibbets, since the ghost of Hamlet's father appeared on the castle battlements in *Hamlet*, 'the stock in trade of horror romanticism has consisted of the inhabitants, properties, and atmosphere of the haunted house' (2002: 99). The haunted house is one of the most consistent and recognisable motifs within horror culture. While the first recognised gothic novel, *The Castle of Otranto*, is set in a castle, the house became central in texts ranging from Poe's *The Fall of the House of Usher* (1839) to Shirley Jackson's *The Haunting of Hill House* (1959). Subsequently, academic surveys of the haunted house have focused on examinations of anxieties over economics, ownership, gender roles, history, and oppression as recurring themes. All of these are present in Eel Marsh House.

The house serves to anchor time and place, but itself is a repository for history that can alienate through the character's distance from and intrusion into it (Smith, 2010). Ghosts offer an opportunity to refute or undermine history. Unsurprisingly, houses are places that register highly on McAndrew's rubric of creepiness (2021). They contain a lot of 'uncertainty' and their physical properties create physiological effects on the human body:

> The agent detection mechanisms discussed earlier are on full alert in the standard haunted house, and for good reason. Things that activate hypervigilance for malevolent forces (whether natural or supernatural) abound in large, drafty old houses: rattling or creaking sounds in upstairs rooms; the sighing and moaning of wind passing through cracks; ragged curtains fluttering in the breeze; echoes; and cold spots. Consequently, it is very easy to imagine that one is not really alone in such a place… Margee Kerr (2015) notes that large old buildings full of rotting wood, exposed ductwork, and other structural defects can produce infrasound and make what is already a creepy experience even spookier. (McAndrew, 2021)

In her survey of contemporary American horror films, Chiho Nakagawa (2018) suggests that the haunted house is the focus for examinations of the modern father and his role and impact within the domestic space. Excluded from the public sphere, the haunted house was traditionally the loci for gothic heroines, and most famous literary works centre on the female psyche in relation to the haunting (and in doing so, call her subjectivity and sanity into question), as with the previous examples.

In *TWIB*, it may be said to be a little of both. Arthur is the traditional breadwinner but clearly is softened by his fatherly love for his family. His work at Crythin Gifford draws him away from his own beloved domestic space. Thus, he invades the domestic space of the Drablow widow, and in the manner of a protagonist in one of M. R. James's ghost stories, his investigations into the past draw recrimination and retribution. Haunted houses, as bastions of private, domestic histories, are perfect receptacles in which to examine the role of the family and familial relations.

Andrew Smith's sharp and detailed analysis of the role of history and identity in the works of Henry James is particularly relevant here for a number of reasons. Smith focuses on the gothic tradition, in which fiction is used 'to animate reality' (2010: 122). Smith points towards James's dual identity as an American and European, who feels equally outside of and 'overwhelmed by' both respective histories, as responsible for the consistent treatment of history as estrangement in his novels (2010: 125). 'Models of identity', Smith argues, are closely related to a sense of place, so estrangement from those places creates a vacuum in which the self is uprooted from security (2010: 140). Those stories which feature ghosts attached to places further illuminate this fractured identity. In particular, the haunted house is the essence of history and to disturb the house is to disturb the dead.

In a similar way, Arthur Kidd is at first distant from the mysterious history of Eel Marsh House, then overwhelmed by it, and finally consumed by it, in a manner similar to the governess in *The Turn of the Screw*. This is more pronounced in the film and not complicated by ambiguity about whether the spectre exists, as is the case in *TTOTS*.

We can learn further from Smith's analysis of Henry James in relation to the text. Smith suggests that 'History is effectively bought but cannot be intellectually owned' (2010: 125). As a disrupter of class, gender, and other values, the woman in black demonstrates this, while the Drablow accumulation of wealth, property, and objects cannot insulate them from the wrath of the vengeful dead any more than poor Keckwick can, for example. Houses are places that intrinsically resurrect the past – disturbing that which is resting.

Gypsies and curses

The presence of gypsies in British culture has often also served to disrupt secure notions of British (or other forms of) identity. Sue Harper has discussed how the Gainsborough melodramas of the 1940s proved distasteful to film critics who were newly minting a set of criteria for 'proper' British national cinema (and by extension, national identity) during and after the Second World War (1994; see also Ellis, 1996). Harper maintains that the depiction of gypsies in Gainsborough films such as *Caravan* (1946) not only presented history as a colourful and exotic pastiche, but also relocated their stories outside of Britain (Europe) and outside of the mainstream (1994; 2009; Spicer, 2009: 297). Gypsy life was thus romanticised but, as Taylor (2011) points out, during the Second World War and other periods of strife or galvanisation of national archetypes, gypsies were scapegoated and reviled for their difference. The term gypsy also had traditional connotations for a woman of easy virtue. Gypsies have fallen, and continue to fall, between these two extremes – 'othered' as not part of the proper societal protocols or equally 'othered' as exotic, romantic outsiders – and further castigated for falling short of this historicised, romantic stereotype (Taylor, 2011; Healey, 2018; Cressey, 2018). In other words, they are caught between two unwanted or impossible polarities.

The gypsy curse is also a prevalent trope within the horror genre, including the recent film *Drag Me to Hell* (2009). Romany gypsies are also visible in Bram Stoker's *Dracula*. Here they are allies and enablers of the Count – and therefore bound within the textual project of dangerous, contaminated foreign invasion (see Arata, 1990). Horror narratives indebted to the vampirism of Stoker's novel have reinforced the association of the vampire and the gypsy, such as Hammer's 1971 film *Vampire Circus*. Their proximity to the supernatural is also manifest in their traditional roles as 'fortune tellers', as in Lewis's *The Monk* or the Universal horror films.

Kneale's inclusion is therefore of particular note and, as discussed in Chapter Two, it is an original contribution to the film. The presence of gypsies disrupts, but perhaps not in the traditional sense described by Harper. Here, the experience of the gypsy is well condensed within a few scenes. Pedlars and itinerants, they are nonetheless stereotypically portrayed as thieves, as the two gypsy girls steal sweets from a market stall. Clearly marked as the woman's next victim, a little girl's leg is pinned under a log which falls from the back of a stricken lorry. Villagers watch passively while the rest of the logs are poised inevitably to crush the girl to death, before Arthur's heroic intervention. A conversation with a local in the pub in the aftermath, in which Arthur downplays his involvement to gauge the local reaction, is revealing: 'Should have left well enough alone. Too many gypsies around – market day brings em' in'.

Several things are important here (see Chapter Six for a discussion of the Victorian attitude to children expressed in the text), but most significant perhaps for the originality of the text is the reversal of the gypsy curse on 'polite society'. It is the gypsy girl who is the target for the death curse of the middle-class woman, not the other way around, which is far more customary. There is no solidarity in the class of outsiders (the wronged woman and ethnic minorities). In fact, the woman's curse has no class or ethnic prejudice, equally targeting the children of lawyers and rich landowners (Pepperell and Toovey) and the working classes (Keckwick) as well as those on the fringes of society. This lack of class distinction or solidarity transgresses the rules of polite society and its careful (and hateful) hierarchies. Therefore, the film goes even further as a horror vehicle in demonstrating how horror and the gothic text are an affront to historical British national identity – an indiscriminate mass of murderous hatred bubbling under the surface of conservative order. Kneale's ending also forgoes the possibility for its restoration.

If the curse has no class distinctions, this is also evident in other ways. Peter Hutchings suggested of the Hammer Horror films that they 'permitted a conservative nostalgia for a fixed social order, one in which those who were powerless were legitimate prey' (Hutchings, 1993: 65). In *TWIB* this is hinted at in Arthur's interaction with the local, who laments Sam Toovey's economic reach: 'Can't match his offers'. The 'order' remains fixed here through the capitalistic hierarchies underpinning Britain's empire that seemingly even the supernatural cannot shift.

In Britain, the historical horror film has been a way of safely relocating the fears of the present to the past and an opportunity for costume and setting to dictate the mood and tone, offering their own distinct visual pleasures. Yet if America has harboured anxieties about its lack of history in comparison to its European forebears, then Britain wrestles with a surfeit of history. Indeed, Britain's reliance on the costume and historical drama to fill film and television screens has habitually been a reason to bemoan its lack of visual integrity, its over-reliance on literary or theatrical culture, and lack of ambition or modern sensibility. It has even led to charged cultural debates over its socio-political function – of conservatism, capitalism, and historical collusion, as in the 'heritage' debates of the 1980s and 1990s (see Higson, 1993).

Yet as Hutchings, Wheatley, and other scholars have indicated, it is precisely these established parameters which have proven fertile ground for gothic and horror texts to examine precisely what lurks underneath the pristine surfaces of the costume drama. For what is horror if not a fear of our own past – of the tensions unresolved, of voices of the abused, disenchanted, and ignored out to claim revenge or parity? Britain may have a longer history of this than America – a small island drowning in the voices of its past discontents. As Robin Wood states, 'the true subject of the horror genre is the struggle for recognition of all that our civilisation represses or oppresses' (in Jancovich, 1996: 1), while for Paul Wells, the horror genre is 'concerned with death and the impacts and effects of the past' (2000: 7). If that repressed past is denser, it stands to reason that its energy is more powerful – its effects more overwhelming.

TWIB was broadcast at a time of social upheaval in the final phases of the Thatcher era, with class distinctions still the subject of intense debate around mobility and exclusion. It was broadcast in the same year as the Community Charge (colloquially, the 'Poll Tax') was introduced, leading to riots, and as the Hillsborough football disaster, which claimed the lives of 97 fans who were also erroneously blamed for it, despite police failings and cover-ups.

It is significant, therefore, that through the central protagonist, Arthur Kidd, *TWIB*'s audience is primed to identify with a member of the professional middle classes. This is complicated somewhat by the working-class background of actor Adrian Rawlins, although he performs the role using received pronunciation. In an interview, Rawlins himself expressed of the character, 'Oh, he's a regular geezer, I've got nothing against him' (in Harper, 2020).

It is once again the authorial intervention of Nigel Kneale that helps distinguish Arthur's liminal status. In the novella, Mr Sweetman (David Ryall) is his boss, but also his friend and confidante. This relationship is extinguished in Kneale's adaptation, and instead it is Sweetman's cowardice and evasiveness that ultimately lead to Kidd's downfall, by sending him to settle Mrs Drablow's estate in his stead. These differences are established in the first scene at the solicitor's office, via several of Kneale's interventions in the story. Firstly, Kidd is seen indulging his two clerks in their childish behaviour, as they discuss the latest Charlie Chaplin film they have seen. Eventually and kindly instructing them to 'settle down', they continue their giggling when Mr Girdler (Robert Hamilton) is heard loudly clearing his throat in the next room.

In the next scene, in Mr Sweetman's office, the correct professional and class protocols are laid out by his boss: 'I've seen you fraternising with the clerks – it won't do. You must cultivate authority'. This cultivation of duty and authority are instructive of the class, imperialist, and masculine virtues that were still a symbol of the inter-war years. It can also be seen in the curt manner in which the peripheral servant to the Kidds, Bessie (Robin Weaver), is treated by Arthur's wife, Stella (Claire Holman). Their son also accuses Bessie of pushing him so that he hit his head on the bathtub and Stella barks orders at her: 'give her to me! Do the nappies'. This creates a focus on Arthur's own paternal/avuncular nature as he treats underlings, animals, and children with kindness and empathy (further evidenced in another of Kneale's touches, as he offers sweets to a little girl on the train – sandwiches in the original script). In Kneale's scripts, Arthur is reading Charles Dickens' *Little Dorrit* on the train; a cautionary tale about child poverty in nineteenth-century London – another of the writer's subtle and economic means of conveying the character's kindness and sense of social welfare. It also contrasts with how working-class characters treat their children, such as the landlord, who describes his potboy, Albert, as 'dratted boy – never there when you need him'.

There is an overall feeling created in the film that people are not just bound by their class and economic position, but imprisoned by them. The woman herself illustrates this point (further elaborated in the next chapter). It is also emphasised by another minor but important character introduced by Kneale – Mr Girdler, a veteran suffering from having been gassed in the First World War. (In the original script, a recording by Mrs Drablow also refers to an actual event that took place during the conflict: 'and I saw a great thing in the night sky. Keckwick says it was a German Zeppelin and it dropped bombs on Great Yarmouth'.) He not only anchors the adaptation in historical context, but also develops Kidd as a character who fights for the common man. Arthur throws his head in his hands when he realises that Girdler is in reception, while his clerks giggle at his hocking. Likewise, Mr Sweetman shows both indifference and contempt towards him: 'who is that person with the appalling sniffle – a client of yours?' Yet Arthur is shown to be sympathetic:

Girdler – 'They don't bloody care. Do you bloody care'?

Arthur – 'Yes, of course I care'.

Arthur is aligned with the liberal section of society that saw the 'Great War' as one of the most destructive human events in history. Girdler represents one of the walking wounded who served, and who remind society viscerally, through their injuries, that the scars of war continue long after the conflict itself. This was also a period in which culture reflected these wounds, such as in the expressionistic horror films of Weimar Germany (for example, *The Cabinet of Dr Caligari*, 1919) and Hollywood – in particular, the anatomically diverse performances of Lon Chaney in films such as *The Shock* in 1923, alongside the anti-war film *All Quiet on the Western Front* of 1930.

Again, Kneale deliberately intervenes to position the adaptation within this specific time period and, through Girdler, to link it with the notion of post-traumatic stress (which Kidd is himself to undergo, like the victims of the First World War) – and furthermore, with the notion of national trauma (continued in the next chapter). Kneale's early *Quatermass* serials and *Nineteen Eighty-Four* both show the literal and metaphorical landscape of post-Second World War trauma in actual and imagined locations as well as in their traumatised protagonists. This, Kneale acknowledged, came from living in post-war London (Murray, 2017: 101–02).

This connection brings us back to the notion of imperial masculinity, and of the Drablows' profiteering from the interrelated martial/mercantile project of the British Empire. It is significant that when Arthur first enters the nursery and catches the ball, as he looks around the room there are several close-up shots of the room's ossified objects – some costumed dolls, a dark-faced Turkish sultan puppet, and some toy soldiers in a fort – as if to connect all these different objects and subjects – war, exoticism, and colonialism – with broken innocence (a common theme of the First World War), as Arthur hears the child's voice for the first time. He then finds a toy soldier placed in his hands before the lights go out. Finding the same toy soldier later in his room at the inn precipitates the horrific manifestation of the woman over him – the point at which his mental breakdown occurs.

Intentionally or otherwise, the connection between war and national trauma is evident. It is interesting that in Kneale's scripts, the toy is not a soldier but a horse – something that links more obviously to the tragic accident. This was likely changed for logistical purposes – fitting more easily into the palm of Arthur's hand and his pocket. (As in the book and the play, it is a rocking horse which causes the noises in the nursery in Kneale's script, not a red ball, as in the final film, echoing both *The Changeling* and *The Shining*.)

Figure 6. Colonial objects in Eel Marsh nursery.

Either way, the toy soldier is a constant reminder of the woman's presence and a precursor to her unleashed rage; but in a larger sense, it is also a constant reminder that the Empire was established and maintained through martial endeavour. Martial endeavour is a source of national pride and triumphant mythology, yet one that masks the horror and violence of its implementation. Buried trauma is the result. Horror texts like *TWIB* give expression to these suppressed realities, and when the trickle turns to a flood, horror is created.

Chapter Six: 'I won't be feared of my own kin': Ghostly Children and Maternal Hatred

Trauma and repressed anxiety are together a leitmotif throughout *TWIB*. This final chapter will continue to explore this theme and how it relates to other major characters who are on the fringes of society in this text – women and children. Scullion indicates that the notion of the 'family' was an ideological battleground in Britain in the 1980s, especially surrounding parental rights and state/familial autonomy, something she suggests is embodied in Hill's novella (2003), but which we can extend to considering in relation to Kneale's adaptation as it appeared as the decade drew its last gasps. Both women and children are important avatars within the gothic and horror genres for the manner in which they represent fears over lack of identity and the notion of the abject within patriarchal societal structures.

Maternal outrage

In Nigel Kneale's one-off drama *Ladies Night* (1986), also directed by Herbert Wise, a 'gentlemen's club' is 'menaced' by women on the one night that they are allowed to attend. The tables are ultimately turned on the distinctly chauvinistic patrons who are uncomfortable with women in their masculine environment. It is certainly a text that may be interpreted as 'feminist' but Kneale's body of work may not necessarily be said to reflect the same. Indeed, his dismissal of Hill's authorship is evident in his attitude to her believing that she could borrow a character surname from the great H. G. Wells (whom Kneale revered) and his disavowal of it. As with most facets of Kneale's career and body of work, his attitude to women (and children) is complex and nuanced and resists simple definitions.

Kneale reveals a sensitivity to, and an awareness of, the unequal status of women in many of his works. In the sadly non-extant TV drama *The Road* (1963), the character Lady Lavinia Hassall states 'The curse of being a woman – no-one believes that what you say is important' (2018 radio adaptation).

Kneale's adaptation of *The Witches* (1966) for Hammer films is particularly significant as it concerns a woman, Gwen Mayfield (Joan Fontaine), haunted by both personal and post-colonial trauma. Alongside this are weak and ineffectual male figures ('the symbols of male authority can only be simulated' according to Hunt, 2002: 90) and a powerful matriarch, Stephanie Bax (Kay Walsh), who uses a hydrogen-bomb analogy to describe the potential power of witchcraft/magic.

In a wider sense, within gothic and horror scholarship, it is noted that the representation of women is paramount in understanding the society that created and informed these texts, not least the nineteenth century, on which Hill's original novella so readily draws. Diane Wallace (2013: 1) indicates that gothic historical fiction functions as a form of meta-history which calls into question the function of history as a public and political concept as opposed to a personal and private one. Occluded by law from public life, the history of women was by necessity personal and private – thus, this marked an erasure from 'history'. Therefore, gothic writing and gothic heroism became a way of reclaiming these histories, symbolic but representative, from expunction: 'fiction has been one of the primary ways in which women writers have written history and written themselves into history' (2013: 2–3).

Unable to own property, and themselves marked as property via the institution of marriage, Wallace suggests that for at least two centuries, women were considered 'civilly dead' – therefore marking their presence and absence as ghostly (2013: 2). Nineteenth-century literature, especially, explored the exclusion and liminal status of women within society. Therefore, there is no shortage of scholarly work on the depictions and significance of women and motherhood in Hill's original novella (and to a lesser extent, the play and 2012 film), and how important connections are made across historical periods by virtue of Hill's self-conscious use of gothic tropes in a text 'rich in intertextual references' (Scullion, 2003: 294).

Scullion, Miquel-Baldellou, and Roberts all suggest that the novella is subversive in providing agency to a character otherwise denied such by her gender, class, and circumstances. For Miquel-Baldellou, 'Jennet thus becomes a single mother at a time when women's sexuality was restricted to marriage, and deviation from the established rules necessarily involved social exclusion' (2021: 168).

Miquel-Baldellou indicates, of the novella, that 'the Victorian past is addressed through a blending of the familiar and the ghostly' (2021: 164), and invokes Julia Brigg's adage that neo-Victorian gothic fiction can be metaphorically interpreted as the personification of the haunting Victorian past (2021: 165). By re-historicising the story and incorporating post-war male trauma, Kneale arguably does something similar here, although, in regaining male authorial control, he would arguably be seen to undermine the subversive energy of Hill and Jennet herself.

Miquel-Baldellou (2021: 169) furthermore equates Jennet in the novella with the trope of the Victorian 'fallen woman' that she also identifies in Victorian gothic literature (Lucy Westenra in *Dracula* and Anne Catherick in *The Woman in White* as exemplars). These characters embody patriarchal fears of uncontrollable women, who are 'often endowed with some sort of symbolic witchcraft which enables them to exert enormous influence on others' (Miquel-Baldellou, 2021: 169). This witchcraft is less symbolic than corporeal in Jennet's case, as Hill absorbs these influences and invigorates them.

An obvious connection with witchcraft is also apparent in the societal tradition of designating older women as witch or hag. Miquel-Baldellou argues that the wasted, emaciated, and prematurely aged figure of Jennet and her wraith suggest this affinity, and her further estrangement from the townsfolk draws even more attention to her marginal and abject status. The notion of madness is also invoked in the case of Jennet, as a reminder that female stridency and independence, and indeed sexuality, were seen as a dangerous malady – a symptom of mental illness (Miquel-Baldellou, 2021: 174).

In a point connecting back to Chapter Four, and haunted and compelling landscapes, Miquel-Baldellou makes the compelling connection between the woman and the places haunted by nineteenth-century gothic women. Water, she suggests, 'symbolically brings back memories of the past' for Rosanna Spearman in *The Moonstone*, for example (The Shivering Sand – Miquel-Baldellou, 2021: 175). There is a connection to the abject, in the amniotic mother figure of Jennet Humfrye and the tidal causeway. Jennet in the novella and Janet in the film are subject to multiple forms of the abject, which may be said to manifest in her destructive enmity and energy.

Scullion also suggests (after Hofer, 1993: 145 in 2003: 293) that the writing and the themes of the novella provided something of a catharsis for Hill after experiencing a miscarriage, linking this to Ellen Moers' thesis that Mary Shelley's traumatic experience of infant mortality similarly informed her writing of *Frankenstein* (in Scullion, 2003: 293). It is clear that the trauma of having a child taken away pervades the text, and provides the emotional core of a story about the persistence of grief, as well as death.

For all commentators, the radical potential of Hill's original novella is bound up in a conflation of silence, a denial of male authority in legal and professional matters, and an inhibition for men to tell the story with any sufficient closure. Gina Wisker reiterates this last point (in Scullion, 2003: 294) noting how a lack of narrative resolution is 'radical'. For Roberts, it is a text that 'resists' the attempts at 'closure' (2014: 130), and for Scullion, Hill's refusal to return to the framing narrative at the beginning of the novella denies a traditional and satisfying conclusion – 'the particular horror is that the ghost is not laid to rest' (2003: 298).

It is the woman's ability to defy the strictures of space and time that makes her an affront to the order and rationality of Arthur's legal mind and prompts his attempt to exorcise her through the act of writing. Patriarchal society is destabilised as the woman does not allow the male storyteller to succeed in restoring order to the text – the feminine authority resists control (Roberts, 2014: 130). D'Arcy invokes Julia Kristeva in that Arthur's attempt to put down in words, and thus lay to rest, his experiences at Eel Marsh House is a failed attempt to separate the abject other from the self so as to reaffirm personal male identity, and by extension, authority (2022: 144).

The reference to the Kristevan abject is significant, as it calls into question both the abject appearance of Janet while alive and dead (pale and wasted) and her murderous link to time and tide. It is worth considering the notion of hydro-feminism at this point. As Neimanis suggests, 'to drink a glass of water is to ingest the ghosts of bodies that haunt that water' (2012: 98). Hydro-feminism embraces the fluid, the temporal and intangible aspects of the human form as opposed to masculine conceptions of the material and the whole – and as such, the untameable and fluid (the sea and water) suggest an extra dimension of horror to male audiences. Janet's link to the tidal causeway, regulated by the waxing and waning of the moon, also suggests a link with the menstrual cycle and potentially even the amniotic – key concepts of the 'abject' that Kristeva ties to masculine fear and disgust. Again, there are important links here with the aquatic presence and provenance of Sadako in *Ringu*. In Hill's story, Eel Marsh House burns to the ground but this fails to stop the curse. In Kneale's adaptation,

Arthur tries once again to cauterise the wound of Janet's curse in his office by setting fire to the Drablow effects, but this masculine, Promethean intervention is once again extinguished by feminine intangibility.

Scullion further suggests that the woman's wrath is also a form of revenge for Arthur's attempts to control the legal documents concerning her past (2003: 297), something that Roberts also notes 'points to the constructedness and vulnerability of patriarchy's reliance on rationality and legality' (2014: 127). Roberts also opines that the breaking of the fourth wall in the theatrical version, whereby the woman also resists the protocols of contemporary space and time by roaming the spaces of the theatre, is further radical in that it 'enhances and expands' the woman's mastery over male authority (2014: 133). The 2012 film version, she argues, also allows for something similar in its use of close-ups (Roberts, 2014: 133).

In making these trenchant observations, the opportunity has been missed (for whatever reasons) to discuss the role of the woman in the TV film, whereby, as discussed at length in Chapter Four, the chilling enmity of the female gaze is arguably even more powerful and prominent in this version, and even more penetrating in its domestic broadcast context as, like *Ringu*'s Sadako again, the woman threatens to break through the fourth wall of the television screen into the audience's home – extending the woman's influence even further.

Figure 7. Janet poised to break through into the domestic realm.

The material presence of the woman in black, dressed in antiquated mourning clothes, also calls into question several points about the imperial nineteenth century, and the role of women in that society, presided over by the matriarchal Queen Victoria. The prevailing contemporaneous image of the Queen is of her in almost perpetual mourning – devoted to the memory of her beloved Prince Albert, during the last 40 years of her life. Despite having nine children with her husband prior to this, a sense of national chasteness is invoked that recalls the previous female monarch who presided over British imperial expansion – the 'virgin Queen', Elizabeth I.

It is worth noting that the Victorian protocol of mourning, part of a larger temporal and societal preoccupation with death, is one that itself suggests female dependence and acquiescence to patriarchal mores also visually manifested by what women had to wear. There were three mourning periods – deep/full mourning, second mourning, and half mourning (muted colours) – which women generally undertook for two years for a widow, during which they were expected not to enter society. It has been suggested that, in addition to the heavy and concealing clothing, which was also uncomfortable and potentially dangerous (colloquially, 'widow's weeds'), this practice was 'essentially keeping them from being comforted by others' (Mendoza, 2018). If Jennet is excluded from society, she simply serves as an avatar, then, for the millions of women in the Victorian era for whom this was a fact. Miquel-Baldellou suggests that the spectral appearance of characters such as Miss Havisham and Lucy Westenra 'underpins the subtle connection established between marriage and death' (2021: 171).

The appearance of the woman in antiquated mourning clothes also serves as yet another 'return of the repressed' – for the imperial period and all that implies, and as yet another reminder that these clothes signify an earlier period of gender imprisonment. That Janet mourns her child and not her partner/husband may be read as another layer of subversion – she wears the uniform but does not follow orders (this was a personal choice for mothers of the deceased in the Victorian era – to mourn indefinitely). As Roberts observes:

> Her power stems from her exaggerated femininity: no language, only female attire and unabated maternal desire. The character is a silhouette, if not a caricature, of nineteenth century femininity, with sweeping black skirts, shawl, bonnet and veil. (2014: 134)

Both D'Arcy and Scullion make connections between the novella and the play and their 1980s context. For D'Arcy, 'the play mirrors the novel's depictions of 1980's cultural horrors' (2022: 137) while being 'produced in a period of Thatcherite commercialisation of culture and the arts' (2022: 138); yet it is 'paradoxical' in that it is also steeped in allusions to the Victorian era as well as being 'deliberately timeless' or otherwise 'indeterminate' in relation to specific time periods (2022: 138–39). Again, this is something that Kneale avoids with his specific historical anchors.

D'Arcy argues that this problematises the text's (play and novella) feminist credentials as it invites the audience to take a post-feminist position of safe historical distancing rather than operating as an instructive comparative to the demonstrable, real-world contemporary contradictions between neo-liberal notions of working women and cuts to child benefits: of 'Victorian values' and free-market capitalism (2022: 137–50).

For Scullion, idealising motherhood within conservative, neo-liberal discourse in this period also highlighted the disparity between ideology and policy (2003: 299–301). Scullion indicates that prior to the introduction of the Children Act, in the same year as *TWIB*'s broadcast, local authorities had the right to take children into social care without consulting the parents (2003: 299). Furthermore, the stereotypical image of the nuclear family (working husband, housewife, and 2.4 children) bore little relation to social reality, representing a mere 13 percent of households (Cairncross in Scullion, 2003: 299). Therefore, Jennet *is* subversive in that she problematises the stereotypical image of the 'good mother' (2003: 301–02) and disrupts the binary of angelic and monstrous (after Gilbert and Gubar, 2000).

Notable are the connections between the woman in black, who snatches children, and longstanding folklore concerning similar figures, both in national and global contexts. As Chainey and Winsham detail, lake and river folklore is 'cruel' and a place of sacrifice – especially of children:

> From the river hags of Northern England – Jenny Greenteeth in Liverpool and Lancashire; Peg Powler of Yorkshire and Durham – to Maria Enganxa, the water hag of Majorca, who haunts wells and watering holes in the same way. All of these creatures warn small children off, and keep them safe from drowning in the dark depths. (2021: 106)

To this list, we could add the Grindylow, the Mexican myth of La Llorona, and the PIFs such as *The Spirit of Dark and Lonely Water* (see Chapter Four), which are direct descendants of many of these folk tales that serve the civic function of signposting danger. Where the woman differs, however, is that a warning is not necessarily enough to subvert and certainly not to assuage her rage. The notion of haunting a well also links back with Japanese culture, not least *Ringu* again, which itself draws upon the myth of *Okiku*, the story of a woman from a lower class who is thrown down a well when she threatens a rich man's standing (Illes, 2010).

Interestingly absent from other iterations, Kneale's original scripts (second and third versions) do suggest that a sacrifice, as with the death of Arthur and his family, might go *some* way to slaking her thirst: 'And the WOMAN watches. The burning hatred has softened a little, as if sated'. Yet, like Sadako and Kayako that follow, Janet's curse continues without resolution: a chastening rebuke to the class and patriarchal boundaries that originally betrayed her.

Haunting and haunted children

The connection between this film and the later cycle of J-horror films is also evident in the encounters between Arthur, the ghostly Nathaniel, and the titular woman. In the *Ju-On* (*Grudge*) series of films, the vengeful spirit of Kayako often appears after the spirit of her son, Toshio, is seen. Likewise, the unseen spirit of Nathaniel prefigures the vengeful spirit of the titular woman in *TWIB*, in particular in the infamous scene in which the woman menaces Arthur in his bed. The dynamic that appears to be in play in both examples is that the child's appearance is something of a trap – appearing playful and 'giggling' in Nathaniel's case, drawing in an innocent protagonist by virtue of their maternal or paternal instincts, to face the wrath of a vengeful and cursed woman whose own maternal instincts have been driven to a demonic intensity.

This is particularly relevant with regards to Arthur Kidd, whom Kneale goes to great lengths to establish as an especially paternal and caring character. It may even be the characteristic that leaves him open and ultimately defenceless to the wrath of Janet. The destruction of the nursery by the woman may reflect her outrage at another challenge for Nathaniel's filial affections, among other potential interpretations. Either way, as Scullion observes, a recurring theme of the text in its many iterations centres on the safety of children (2003: 292). The links between the TV film and the public information films of the 1970s discussed in Chapter Four, as well as the links to folkloric figures of child-snatchers mentioned above, indicate that this is not necessarily a time-specific dimension but could also have specific temporal contours, as evidenced by Scullion and D'Arcy's discussion of politicised motherhood in the 1980s.

Ghostly and malevolent children take on a particular significance in post-war British film. The rise of the teenager and youth culture in the 1950s and 1960s, and latterly of the 'counter-culture', created opportunities for generational fears and attendant folk devils, prominent examples being the fears surrounding 'teddy boys' and 'mods and rockers' (Cohen, 1980).

The 1960s and 1970s saw a cultural connection between children and devilry (for example, in *Rosemary's Baby*, *The Exorcist*, and *The Omen*, among others) while teenage girls were connected with destructive psychic energy (*Carrie*, 1976; *Don't go to Sleep*, 1982). Nigel Kneale's 'Special Offer', an episode of his anthology series *Beasts*, starring Pauline Quirke as a sexually frustrated teenager with psychic powers, was broadcast in October 1976, several months before Brian de Palma's adaptation of the Stephen King bestseller was released in the UK (January 1977) and even before its Hollywood debut (November 1977).

Indeed, much has been made of Kneale's supposed ambivalence to children and youth cultures, a position he seemed to affirm with his depiction of the violent and recidivist Planet People in *The Quatermass Conclusion* (ITV, 1979) as well as in *Bam! Pow! Zapp!* and the un-filmed *The Big, Big Giggle*. Kneale even confirmed this himself with his preoccupation with destructive youth cults (Interview for 'A weekend with A Living Legend, Nigel Kneale' dossier, 1999; *Quatermass* Synopsis, Archives MS11631).

However, Kneale's ambivalence seemed to be aimed at youth, rather than children, for whose welfare he genuinely appeared to care – famously believing *Doctor Who* to be too disturbing for child audiences (Murray, 2017: 163). This is also evident in Kneale's adaptation of Hill's story. As discussed, Arthur Kidd is characterised as a naturally paternal soul. These attitudes, unconsciously or not, also reveal Kneale's approach to the slow-burning, emotive (with a dash of occasional humour), and carefully crafted terror of his adaptation of the tale.

Bacon and Ruickbie note that due to their designation in nineteenth-century imperial masculine culture, 'the child was viewed as a point of potential societal weakness and open to outside influence and moral corruption' (2020: 3). It is interesting to compare this with the discussion of the woman's liminal, ghostly, and abject presence within patriarchal cultures.

It is also interesting that the film chooses to provide Nathanial with only a voice, and not a physical manifestation. This is a potentially subversive characterisation attendant to that of the woman herself – both marginalised, they arguably take on greater significance and visibility/audibility in death. Victorian children were famously designated to 'be seen and not heard', but this dichotomy is deliberately reversed here, giving powerful voice and agency to the marginalised figure of the child.

It may also be significant to ponder that, had Nathaniel lived, his fate may have been amongst the mud of the trenches of the First World War and not amongst the mud of the causeway – the fate of many a child of the Empire.

Conclusion

If we have achieved nothing else with this book, we hope to have shown, at least, that televisual texts demand the same level of attention, investigation, and interrogation as their cinematic counterparts and that doing so will yield rich results. They are just as fondly remembered and, at times, just as swiftly forgotten as horror films once were. If horror films were once dismissed by critics then TV horror films were doubly denigrated as an inferior type of content experienced on an inferior cultural form. *TWIB*'s liminal status as a text in-between helps to elucidate some of these differences, and indeed, fallacies. The subtle crafting of Kneale and Wise, discussed here, suggests the authorial agency in creating televisual horror.

Figure 8. Conclusive finale as Arthur and family are fatally drawn into the woman's web.

We hope to have opened up, in some way, the path for others to consider the vast range of made-for-TV horror films as subjects more than suitable for stand-alone consideration for their rich cultural significance. Jonathan Miller's *Whistle and I'll Come to You* (1968), Kneale's own *The Stone Tape* (1972), the controversial but superlative *Ghostwatch* (1992), and of course, any of the revered *A Ghost Story for Christmas* strand from the 1970s onwards are just a handful of examples in a British context before we even consider America and other televisual-content-producing cultures – or indeed series (*Dead of Night*), miniseries (*Salem's Lot*), anthology series, live specials, one-offs, animations, and others.

Yet, we also hope to have shown that *TWIB* is a significant text, with wide-reaching social and cultural significance. It is at once a text in conversation with its literary origins and concomitant iterations in different forms; in conversation with the alleged differences and similarities between film and television; a text which is part of a global semiotic exchange of ideas within the horror genre yet at the same time which reveals much of its spatial and temporal context of production – the cracks and fissures within British history.

Susan Hill was said to be dissatisfied with *TWIB* but Kneale's links between trauma and the First World War may well have influenced her to set *The Woman in Black: Angel of Death* (2014) in the Second World War, and feature a character with PTSD. Either way, Kneale's adaptation will continue to live on as a lesser-seen, relatively underappreciated masterpiece of storytelling and directorial economy, of finely drawn and nuanced performance, of expert sound design and practical effects, but perhaps most importantly of all, of exquisite terror.

Bibliography

Books

Abbott, Stacy, and Lorna Jowett (2013) *TV Horror: Investigating the Dark Side of the Small Screen*, London: I. B. Tauris.

Benson, E. F. (2012) 'The Dance', in *Night Terrors: The Ghost Stories of E. F. Benson*, Ware: Wordsworth Editions, 569–80.

Brontë, Charlotte (1999) *Jane Eyre*, Ware: Wordsworth.

Brown, Steven T. (2018) *Japanese Horror and the Transnational Cinema of Sensations*, Cham: Springer.

Carroll, Lewis (1992) *Alice in Wonderland*, New York; London: W. W. Norton & Co.

Caughie, J. (2000) *Television Drama: Realism, Modernism and British Culture*, Oxford: Oxford University Press.

Chainey, Dee, and Willow Winsham (2021) *Treasury of Folklore: Sea and Rivers, Sirens, Selkies and Ghost Ships*, London: Batsford.

Chion, Michael (2009) *Film, a Sound Art* (trans. Claudia Gorbman), New York: Columbia.

Cohen, Stanley (1980) *Folk Devils and Moral Panics: the Creation of the Mods and Rockers*, Oxford: Martin Robertson.

Collins, Wilkie (1966) *The Moonstone*, Harmondsworth: Penguin.

—— (1994) *The Woman in White*, London: Penguin.

Cook, Michael (2014) *Detective Fiction and the Ghost Story: The Haunted Text*, London and New York: Palgrave Macmillan.

Cressey, David (2018) *Gypsies: An English History*, Oxford: Oxford University Press.

Dickens, Charles (1979) *Little Dorrit*, Oxford: Clarendon Press.

—— (2009) 'The Signalman', in *Complete Ghost Stories: Charles Dickens*, Ware: Wordsworth.

Dimendberg, Edward (2004) *Film Noir and the Spaces of Modernity*, Cambridge, MA: Harvard University Press.

Doyle, Arthur Conan (2009) *The Hound of the Baskervilles: Another Adventure of Sherlock Holmes*, London: Penguin.

Eliot, George (1998) *The Mill on the Floss*, Oxford: Oxford University Press.

Frank, Alan G. (1974) *The Movie Treasury: Horror Movies*, Cathay Books.

Gilbert, Sandra M., and Susan Gubar (2000) *The Madwoman in the Attic: The Woman Writer and the Nineteenth Century Imagination*, New Haven: Yale University Press.

Golding, William (2005) *The Lord of the Flies*, London: Faber.

Gray, Thomas (1926) *Elegy Written in a Country Churchyard*, in M. G. Edgar and Eric Chilman (eds), *A Treasury of Verse for School and Home*, London: George G. Harrap & Co. Ltd, 426–30.

Hand, Richard J. (2014) *Listen in Terror: British Horror Radio from the Advent of Broadcasting to the Digital Age*, Manchester: Manchester University Press.

Handley, Sasha (2015) *Visions of an Unseen World: Ghost Beliefs and Ghost Stories in Eighteenth Century England*, Abingdon: Routledge.

Harper, Sue (1994) *Picturing the Past: The Rise and Fall of the British Costume Film*, London: BFI.

Hayward, Philip (2009) *Terror Tracks: Music, Sound and Horror Cinema*, London: Equinox.

Hill, Susan (1961) *The Enclosure*, London: Hutchinson.

—— (1973) *I'm the King of the Castle*, London: Penguin.

—— (1973) *Strange Meeting*, London: Penguin.

—— (1976) *The Bird of Night*, London: Penguin.

—— (1980) *A Change for the Better*, London: Penguin.

—— (1983) *The Woman in Black*, London: Penguin.

—— (2000) *The Albatross*, London: Penguin.

—— (2009) *The Beacon*, London: Vintage.

—— (2012) *The Man in the Picture: A Ghost Story*, London: Profile Books.

—— (2013) *Dolly: A Ghost Story*, London: Profile Books.

—— (2017) *The Travelling Bag and Other Ghostly Stories*, London: Profile Books.

—— (2018) *From the Heart*, London: Profile Books.

—— (2023) *The Small Hand*, London: Vintage.

Hutcheon, Linda (2006) *A Theory of Adaptation*, Abingdon: Routledge.

Hutchings, Peter (1993) *Hammer and Beyond: The British Horror Film*, Manchester: Manchester University Press.

—— (2001) *Terence Fisher*, Manchester: Manchester University Press.

Illes, Judika (2010) *The Encyclopedia of Spirits: The Complete Guide to the Magic of Fairies, Genies, Demons, Ghosts, Gods and Goddesses*, Harper Collins: New York.

Jacobs, W. W. (1995) *The Monkey's Paw*, Charlottesville: Generic NL Freebook Publisher.

James, Henry (2001) *The Turn of the Screw*, in *Ghost Stories of Henry James*, Ware: Wordsworth, 175–266.

James, M. R. (1992) 'Lost Hearts', in *M. R. James: Collected Ghost Stories*, Ware: Wordsworth Editions Limited, 20–35.

—— (1992) 'The Mezzotint', in *M. R. James: Collected Ghost Stories*, Ware: Wordsworth Editions Limited, 36–53.

—— (1992) 'Oh, Whistle, and I'll Come to You, My Lad', in *M. R. James: Collected Ghost Stories*, Ware: Wordsworth Editions Limited, 120–50.

—— (1992) 'The Stalls of Barchester Cathedral', in *M. R. James: Collected Ghost Stories*, Ware: Wordsworth Editions Limited, 268–88.

Jancovich, Mark (1996) *Rational Fears: American Horror Genre in the 1950s*, Manchester: Manchester University Press.

Jerome, Jerome K. (2020) *Three Men in a Boat*, Oxford: Oxford University Press.

Johnson, Catherine (2005) *Telefantasy*, London: BFI.

Johnston, Derek (2015a) *Haunted Seasons: Ghost Stories for Christmas and Horror for Halloween*, London: Palgrave.

King, Stephen (2011) *Carrie*, London: Hodder.

Lerner, Neil (2010) *Music in the Horror Film: Listening to Fear*, London: Routledge.

Lewis, M. G. (2008) *The Monk*, Oxford: Oxford University Press.

Marsh, Richard (2004) *The Beetle*, Holicong: Wildside Press.

Maynard, Christopher (1977) *The World of the Unknown: All About Ghosts*, London: Usborne Publishing.

Mosse, Kate (2014) 'The Revenant', in *The Mistletoe Bride and Other Haunting Tales*, London: Orion, 175–94.

Muir, John Kenneth (2012) *Horror Films of the 1970s*, Jefferson NC: McFarland.

Murphy, Patrick J. (2018) *Medieval Studies and the Ghost Stories of M. R. James*, Pennsylvania: Penn State University Press.

Murray, Andy (2017) *Into the Unknown: The Fantastic Life of Nigel Kneale*, Headpress.

Newcomb, Horace (1974) *TV: The Most Popular Art*, New York: Anchor/Doubleday.

O'Connor, Sean (2022) *The Haunting of Borley Rectory: The Story of a Ghost Story*, London: Simon and Schuster.

Paver, Michelle (2019) *Wakenhyrst*, London: Head of Zeus.

Poe, Edgar Allen (1992) *The Fall of the House of Usher and Other Tales*, London: Marshall Cavendish.

Roberts, Jerry (2009) *Encyclopedia of Television Film Directors*, Scarecrow Press.

Sayers, Dorothy L. (2016) *The Nine Tailors: A Lord Peter Wimsey Mystery*, London: Hodder Paperbacks.

Schafer, Murray (2005) 'Open Ears', in Michael Bull and Les Black (eds), *The Auditory Culture Reader*, 25–40.

Sconce, Jeffrey (2000) *Haunted Media: Electronic Presence from Telegraphy to Television*, Durham and London: Duke University Press.

Shakespeare, William (1992) *Hamlet*, Ware: Wordsworth Editions Limited.

—— (1994) *The Tempest*, London: Routledge.

Shelley, Mary (1999) *Frankenstein*, Ware: Wordsworth.

Smith, Andrew (2010) *The Ghost Story 1840–1920: A Cultural History*, Manchester: Manchester University Press.

Stoker, Bram (1903) *The Jewel of the Seven Stars*, at Project Gutenberg.

—— (2014) *Dracula*, London: Titan Books.

Suzuki, Koji (2010) *Ring*, London: Harper Collins.

Wallace, Diane (2013) *Female Gothic Histories: Gender, History and the Gothic*, Cardiff: University of Wales Press.

Walpole, Horace (2001) *The Castle of Otranto*, London: Penguin.

Wells, H. G. (2017) *The Island of Doctor Moreau*, Oxford: Oxford University Press.

Wells, Paul (2000) *The Horror Genre: From Beelzebub to Blair Witch*, New York: Wallflower Press.

Wheatley, Helen (2006) *Gothic Television*, Manchester: Manchester University Press.

Articles

Allen, S. (2008) British cinema at the seaside: the limits of liminality, *Journal of British Television*, 5: 1, 53–71.

Arata, Stephen D. (1990) The Occidental Tourist: 'Dracula' and the Anxiety of Reverse Colonization, *Victorian Studies*, 33: 4, 621–45.

Bacon, Helena, and Adam Whybray (2021) The Lies of the Land: The Alluvial Formalities of Gothic East Anglia, *Gothic Studies*, 23: 2, 217–32.

Burkhard, Denise (2016) Between Madness, Malice and Marginalization: Reading the Ghost of Jennet Humfrye in Susan Hill's *The Woman in Black* in the context of Trauma Theory, *Supernatural Studies*, 3: 2, 9–20.

Cardwell, Sarah (2015) A Sense of Proportion: Aspect Ratio and the Framing of Television Space, *Critical Studies in Television*, 10: 3, Autumn, 83–100.

D'Arcy, Jeanette (2022) 'We can believe he does not see her, nor know she's there': Erasure and *The Woman in Black*, *Gothic Studies*, 24: 2, 137–50.

Fisher, Mark (2012) What is Hauntology?, *Film Quarterly*, 66: 1, 16–24.

Fryers, Mark (2020) Horrific In-betweenness: Spatial and Temporal Displacement and British Society in 1970s Children's Supernatural Television, *Supernatural Studies*, 6: 2, 30–58.

—— (2021a) The Haunted Waters of British Film and Television: Nation, Environment and Horror, *Gothic Nature*, II, 131–55.

Halberstam, Judith (1993) Technologies of Monstrosity: Bram Stoker's *Dracula*, *Victorian Studies*, 36: 3, 333–52.

Healey, Jonathan (2018) 'Gypsies: An English History' by David Cressy review, *History Today*, 68: 10, October 10, Available at: https://www.historytoday.com/archive/review/gypsies-english-history-david-cressy-review.

Hutchings, Peter (2004) Uncanny Landscapes in British Film and Television, *Visual Culture in Britain*, 5: 2, 27–40.

James, M. R. (1922) Twelve Medieval Ghost-Stories, *The English Historical Review*, 37: 147, 413–22.

Johnston, Derek (2015b) Breaking the intimate screen: pre-recording, special effects and the aesthetics of early British television, *Critical Studies in Television*, 10: 3, 53–66.

Liggins, Emma (2022) 'Meddling with Sorcery': Hypnotism, the Occult and the Return of the Forsaken Women in the 1890s Ghost Stories of Lettice Galbraith, *Women's Writing*, 29: 2, 177–95.

Mackenzie, Amy (2017) 12 reasons why Rachel Portman is an inspirational film composer, *Classic FM*, Available at: https://www.classicfm.com/composers/rachel-portman/reasons-we-love-rachel-portman/.

McAndrew, F. T. (2021) The Psychology, Geography and Architecture of Horror: How Place Creep Us Out, *Evolutionary Studies in Imaginative Culture*, 4: 2, Available at: https://doi.org/10.26613/esic.4.2.189.

Meinel, Larina Sue, and Claudia Bullerjahn (2022) More horror due to specific music placement? Effects of film music on psychophysiological responses to a horror film, *Psychology of Music*, 50: 6, 1837–52.

Michlin, Monica (2012/2023) The Haunted House in Contemporary Filmic Literary Gothic Narratives of Trauma, *Transatlantica*, https://journals.openedition.org/transatlantica/5933.

Miquel-Baldellou, Marta (2021) 'As Soon as Ever She Died, the Hauntings Began': Revisiting the Victorian Fallen Woman as a Gothic Archetype in Susan Hill's *The Woman in Black*, *Ex-Centric Narratives: Journal of Anglophone Literature, Culture and Media*, 5, 164–83.

Nakagawa, Chiho (2018) Dangers Inside the Home: Rereading Haunted House Films from a Gothic Perspective, *The Journal of American and Canadian Studies*, 35, 75–96.

Panos, Leah and Stephen Lacey (2015) Editorial: The Spaces of Television, *Critical Studies in Television*, 10: 3, 1–4, Available at: https://doi.org/10.7227/CST.10.3.1.

Roberts, Robin (2014) Gender, Adaptation and Authorship – Three Decades of *The Woman in Black*, *Studies in Theatre and Performance*, 34: 2, 126–39.

Scullion, Val (2003) Susan Hill's *The Woman in Black*: Gothic Horror for the 1980s, *Women: A Cultural Review*, 14: 3, 292–305.

Simpson, Jacqueline (2003) Repentant soul or walking corpse? Debatable apparitions in medieval England, *Folklore*, 114: 3, 389–402.

Sterritt, David (2018) Fuller, Fisher, and the Art of the B-Movie Auteur, *Quarterly Review of Film and Video*, 35: 7, 737–40.

Stone, Nora (2017) Small Screen to Big Screen: Made for TV Movies in American and International Cinemas, *Historical Journal of Film, Radio and Television*, 37: 4, 615–29.

Straight, Alyssa (2017) Giving Birth to a New Nation; Female Mediation and the Spread of Textual Knowledge in *Dracula, Victorian Literature and Culture*, 45, 381–94.

Taylor, Becky (2011) Britain's Gypsy Travellers: A People on the Outside, *History Today*, 61: 6, June, Available at: https://www.historytoday.com/archive/britains-gypsy-travellers-people-outside.

Trevor, Caitlyn, Luc H. Arnal, and Sacha Frühholz (2020) Terrifying Film Music Mimics Alarming Acoustic Feature of Human Screams, *The Journal of the Acoustical Society of America*, 147: 6, 540–45.

BOOK CHAPTERS

Armitt, Lucie (2016) 'Ghost-Al Erosion: Beaches and the Supernatural in Two Stories by M. R. James', in Lisa Fletcher (ed.), *Popular Fiction and Spatiality: Reading Genre Settings*, London: Palgrave Macmillan, 95–108.

––– (2017) 'Haunted Landscapes', in Scott Brewster and Luke Thurston (eds), *The Routledge Handbook to the Ghost Story*, London: Routledge, 291–300.

Bacon, Simon, and Leo Ruickbie (2020) 'Introduction', in Bacon and Ruickbie (eds), *The Cultural Construction of Monstrous Children: Essays on Anomalous Children from 1595 to the Present Day*, London and New York: Anthem Press, 1–19.

Edmundson, Melissa (2017) 'Women Writers and Ghost Stories', in Scott Brewster and Luke Thurston (eds), *The Routledge Handbook to the Ghost Story*, London: Routledge, 69–77.

Ellis, John (1996) 'The Quality Film Adventure: British Critics and the Cinema 1942-1948', in Andrew Higson (ed.), *Dissolving Views: Key Writings on British Cinema*, London: Continuum, 66–93.

Fryers, Mark (2021b) '"It's not ghosts it's history": The Sonic Tradition of British Horror Television', in Stacey Abbott and Lorna Jowett (eds), *Global TV Horror*, Cardiff: University of Wales Press, 33–50.

Fryers, Mark, and Marcus K. Harmes (forthcoming) 'Nigel Kneale and Megaliths', in Derek Johnston (ed.), *Nigel Kneale and Horror*, Liverpool: Liverpool University Press.

Harper, Sue (2009) 'Bonnie Prince Charlie Revisited: British Costume Film in the 1950s', in Robert Murphy (ed.), *The British Cinema Book*, 3rd Edition, London: BFI, 276–85.

Higson, Andrew (1993) 'Re-presenting the National Past: Nostalgia and Pastiche in the Heritage Film', in Lester Friedman (ed.), *Fires Were Started: British Cinema and Thatcherism*, Minnesota: University of Minnesota Press.

Hunt, Leon (2002) 'Necromancy in the UK: witchcraft and the occult in British horror', in S. Chibnall and Julian Petley (eds), *British Horror Cinema*, London; New York: Routledge, 82–98.

Krzywinska, Tanya (2007) 'Lurking Beneath the Skin: British Pagan Landscapes in Popular Culture', in Robert Fish (ed.), *Cinematic Countrysides*, Manchester: Manchester University Press, 75–90.

Matthew, H. C. G. (1993) 'The Liberal Age (1851–1914)', in Kenneth O. Morgan (ed.), *The Oxford Illustrated History of Britain*, Oxford: Oxford University Press, 463–522.

McNaughton, Douglas (2018) '"Visible" and "Invisible" Performance: Framing Performance in 1970s Television Drama', in Tom Cantrell and Christopher Hogg (eds), *Exploring Television Acting*, London: Bloomsbury, 29–46.

Neimanis, Astrida (2012) 'Hydrofeminism: Or, On Becoming a Body of Water', in Henriette Gunkel, Chrysanthi Nigianni, and Fanny Söderbäck (eds), *Undutiful Daughters: Mobilizing Future Concepts, Bodies and Subjectivities in Feminist Thought and Practice*, New York: Palgrave Macmillan, 96–115.

Punter, David (2001) 'Introduction: The Ghost of a History', in Punter (ed.), *A Companion to the Gothic*, Oxford: Blackwell Publishing, viii–xiv.

Spicer, Andrew (2009) 'Male Stars, Masculinity and British Cinema, 1945–60', in Robert Murphy (ed.), *The British Cinema Book*, 3rd Edition, London: BFI, 296–303.

Tibbetts, John C. (2002) 'The old dark house: the architecture of ambiguity in The Turn of the Screw and The Innocents,' in Steve Chibnall and Julian Petley (eds), *British Horror Cinema*, London and New York: Routledge, 99–116.

Conference Papers

Cottis, D. (2024) 'M. R. James and Nigel Kneale', *Sequestered Places, Heaving Seas: The Life and Works of M. R. James*, University of Suffolk, 30 April 2024.

Newspaper and Periodical Sources

Anime News Network (no date), Koji Suzuki Biography, available at: https://www.animenewsnetwork.com/encyclopedia/people.php?id=19052.

Birmingham Mail (1989) 14 December, p. 28.

Dugdale, John (1989) 'Watching Week', *The Listener*, 21 December, p. 48.

Harper, Rachel (2020) 'The Woman in Black: An interview with Adrian Rawlins', SciFiNow, 7 August, Accessed 14 September 2023, available at: https://www.scifinow.co.uk/interviews/the-woman-in-black-interview-with-adrian-rawlins/.

Holliss, Richard (1983) 'Nigel Kneale on Halloween III', *Starburst*, 4: 11, July, pp. 30–33.

Kipling, Rudyard (1899) 'The White Man's Burden', *McClure's Magazine*, 12 (1899), pp. 290–91.

Last, Richard (1989) *The Daily Telegraph*, 27 December, p. 14.

Male, Andrew (2020) 'The Woman in Black: Why did Britain's Scariest Horror Film Disappear?', *The Guardian*, 7 August, available at: https://www.theguardian.com/film/2020/aug/07/the-woman-in-black-britain-horror-film-herbert-wise.

Mendoza, Marilyn A. (2018) 'Death and Mourning Practices in the Victorian Age', *Psychology Today*, 8 December, Available at: https://www.psychologytoday.com/gb/blog/understanding-grief/201812/death-and-mourning-practices-in-the-victorian-age.

The Nottingham Evening Post (1989) 23 December, p. 56.

Purser, Philip (1989) *The Daily Telegraph*, 22 December, p. 19.

Saynor, James (1990) 'Tents and Tenterhooks', *The Listener*, 4 January.

Screen International (1989) 'Notes', 4 February, p. 73.

The Stage (1988) 7 January, p. 10.

Stoddart, Patrick (1989) *The Sunday Times*, 24 December, p. 23.

Stubbs, David (2011) 'Why I, Claudius should be remade', *The Guardian*, 13 June.

The Times (1989) 23 December, p. 36.

Totaro, D. (2000) 'The "Ring" Master: Interview with Hideo Nakata', *Offscreen*, 4: 3, Available at: https://offscreen.com/view/hideo_nakata?/new_offscreen/nakata.html.

The Visitor (1989) 21 December, p. 29.

Archives

Interview for 'A weekend with A Living Legend, Nigel Kneale' dossier, 1999, Kneale Archives, MS11631.

The Nigel Kneale Archive Collection – MS11631.

The Woman in Black, Script Draft One, Two and Three, 1988–1989, MS11631.

Interviews

Interview with Bill Kirk, April 2023.

Interview with Martin Kempton, August 2023.

Other Media

Campbell, Ramsay (2012) *Lost Hearts*, BBC Ghost Story for Christmas DVD Viewing Notes, pp. 14–16.

Easterbrook, Adam (2012) *A Warning to the Curious*, BBC Ghost Story for Christmas DVD Viewing Notes, pp. 10–13.

Pixley, Andrew (2020) *The Woman in Black* DVD Viewing Notes.

The Woman in Black DVD Extras.

THEATRE

The Woman in Black, d. Stephen Mallatratt.

RADIO

The Road (2018) d. Charlotte Riches.

The Woman in Black (1993) d. John Strickland.

You Must Listen (1952).

FILM AND TELEVISION

Afterdeath (2015).

Alfie (1966).

All Quiet on the Western Front (1930).

The Amityville Horror (1979).

Annihilation (2018).

Armchair Theatre (1956–74) TV.

The Ash Tree (1975) TV.

The Asphyx (1972).

The Astonished Heart (1950).

Beasts (1976) TV.

Beasts: Buddy Boy (1976) TV.

Beasts: During Barty's Party (1976) TV.

Beasts: Special Offer (1976) TV.

The Beetle (1919).

The Bill (1984–2010) TV.

The Birthday Party (1968).

Bless Me, Father (1978–81) TV.

Boon (1986–92) TV.

Brief Encounter (1945).

The Cabinet of Dr Caligari (1919).

Caravan (1946).

Carrie (1976).

The Changeling (1980).

Churchill's People (1975) TV.

Class Act (1994) TV.

Colditz (1972–74) TV.

Crooked House (2008) TV.

The Curse of Frankenstein (1957).

Dad's Army (1968–77) TV.

The Dark Eyes of London (1939).

David Copperfield (1976) TV.

The Day After (1983) TV.

Dead of Night (1945).

Dead of Night (1972) TV.

Doctor Who (1963–89) TV.

Doctor Who: The Dæmons (1971) TV.

Dogged (2017).

Don't Be Afraid of the Dark (1973) TV.

Don't Be Afraid of the Dark (2010).

Don't Go to Sleep (1982) TV.

Don't Look Now (1973).

Doomwatch (1972).

Dracula (1977).

Drag Me to Hell (2009).

Duel (1971).

Elizabeth R. (1971) TV.

The Entertainer (1960).

The Exorcist (1973).

First Night: The Road (1963) TV.

Frenzy (1972).

Gargoyles (1972) TV.

The Gathering Storm (1974) TV.

Ghost Stories (2017).

Ghosts of Borley Rectory (2021).

Ghostwatch (1992) TV.

The Ghoul (1932).

Halloween (1978).

Halloween III: Season of the Witch (1982).

Hammer House of Horror (1980) TV.

Hellraiser (1987).

A History of Horror with Mark Gatiss (2010) TV.

HMS Defiant (1962).

I, Claudius (1976).

The Ice House (1978) TV.

The Innocents (1961).

Julius Caesar (1979) TV.

Ju-On: The Grudge (2002).

The League of Gentleman (1999–2017) TV.

Look Back in Anger (1959).

Lost Hearts (1973) TV.

The Lovers! (1973).

Mystery and Imagination (1966) TV.

Mystery and Imagination: The Open Door (1966) TV.

Night of the Big Heat (1967).

The Night of the Demon (1957).

Night of the Eagle (1962).

Night of the Living Dead (1968).

Night Mail (1936).

The Night Stalker (1972) TV.

Nineteen Eighty-Four (1954) TV.

The Norman Conquests (1977) TV.

The Omen (1976).

The Others (2001).

Out of the Unknown: The Chopper (1971) TV.

The Pallisers (1974–75) TV.

Pied Piper (1989).

Play for Today: Robin Redbreast (1970) TV.

Poirot (1989–2013) TV.

Poltergeist (1982).

Pope John Paul II (1984) TV.

Possum (2018).

Quatermass and the Pit (1967).

The Quatermass Conclusion (1979) TV.

The Quatermass Experiment (1953) TV.

The Quatermass Xperiment (1955).

The Reeds (2010).

Remember Me (2014) TV.

Reunion at Fairborough (1985) TV.

The Rezort (2015).

Ringu (1998).

Room 13 (1961) TV.

Rumpole of the Bailey (1978–92) TV.

Sadako (2012).

Saint Maude (2019).

Salem's Lot (1979) TV.

Satan's School for Girls (1973) TV.

Satan's Triangle (1975) TV.

The Screaming Woman (1972) TV.

Screen Two: Do Not Disturb (1991) TV.

Sharpe's Gold (1995) TV.

The Shock (1923).

The Signalman (1976) TV.

Skokie (1981) TV.

So Long at the Fair (1950).

Softly, Softly: Task Force (1969–76) TV.

The Spirit of Dark and Lonely Water (1973).

The Stalls of Barchester (1971) TV.

Stanley and the Women (1991) TV.

Stigma (1977) TV.

The Stone Tape (1972) TV.

Studio '64: The Crunch (1964) TV.

Sunday-Night Theatre: Nineteen Eighty-Four (1954) TV.

Sunday-Night Theatre: Wuthering Heights (1953) TV.

Supernatural (1977) TV.

Tales of Mystery and Imagination (1966) TV.

Threads (1984) TV.

A Touch of Frost (1992–2010) TV.

The Treasure of Abbot Thomas (1974) TV.

Unhappy Birthday (2011).

The Uninvited (1997).

Unnatural Causes: Ladies Night (1986) TV.

Vampire Circus (1971).

Van der Valk (1972–92) TV.

Voices (1973).

A Warning to the Curious (1972) TV.

The Web (1951).

The Wednesday Play: Bam! Pow! Zapp! (1969) TV.

Whistle and I'll Come to You (1968) TV.

Whistle and I'll Come to You (2010) TV.

The Wicker Man (1973).

Widow's Walk (2019).

The Witches (1966).

The Witchfinder General (1968).

Wives and Daughters (1971) TV.

The Wolf Man (1941).

The Wolfman (2010).

The Woman in Black (1989).

The Woman in Black (2012).

The Woman in Black: Angel of Death (2014).

Writer's Retreat (2015).